Fenians and Fenianism

CENTENARY ESSAYS EDITED BY MAURICE HARMON

SCEPTER BOOKS   DUBLIN

EDITED BY MAURICE HARMON
With an Introduction by Donal McCartney
University of Washington Press
Seattle

Technical and legal information

FENIANS AND FENIANISM, first published in 1968
by Scepter Publishers Limited, Dublin, is
based on the Winter 1967 issue of *University
Review.*

First published by the University of Washington
Press, 1970, by arrangement with Scepter
Publishers Limited
Library of Congress Catalog Card Number 79-103321
Printed in the Republic of Ireland

For my mother
and in memory of my father

Contents

Contributors

MAURICE HARMON. Lectures in English at University College, Dublin. Has been a Teaching Fellow at Harvard University and Professor of English at the University of Notre Dame. Dr. Harmon has lectured widely in the United States. He is Irish Secretary of the American Committee for Irish Studies. His publications include *Seán Ó Faoláin* (1967) and *Modern Irish Literature* (1967) and articles in scholarly journals on both sides of the Atlantic. He is editor of the *Irish University Review*.

DONAL McCARTNEY. Lecturer in Modern Irish History, University College, Dublin. Has contributed to books of historical essays, including *The Course of Irish History* and *Leaders and Men of the Easter Rising*. Published articles in *Irish Historical Studies* and *Irish Ecclesiastical Record*.

SEÁN Ó SUILLEABHÁIN. Archivist to the Irish Folklore Commission. Author of several books on aspects of Irish folklore, including *A Handbook of Irish Folklore: The Types of Irish Folktale* (1963), *Irish Wake Amusements* (1966). Edited and translated *Folktales of Ireland* (1966).

NORMAN McCORD. Lecturer in Modern History at the University of Newcastle upon Tyne. Received his Ph.D. from Cambridge. Has published *The Anti-Corn Law League*.

MALCOLM BROWN. Professor of English, University of Washington. Has published *George Moore: A Reconsideration*.

HEREWARD SENIOR. Associate Professor of History at McGill University, Montreal. Has published *Orangeism in Ireland and Britain 1795-1836* (1966), and articles in *Thought, Canadian Historical Review*, and *The New Review*.

ROBIN B. BURNS. Lecturer in History, Sir George Williams University, Montreal.

MICHAEL HURST. Fellow of St. John's College, Oxford. Literary editor of the *Oxford Magazine*. Has published *Parnell and Irish Nationalism*.

Introduction

THE essays in this book deal with a revolutionary movement that began simultaneously in Dublin and New York during the late 1850s. It affected British, Irish, American, and Canadian politics during the following couple of decades. And it proved to be a pervasive and continuing influence on Irish life and literature.

The book should prove of value, however, not only to students of Irish, Irish-American, British, or Canadian history, but to all who are interested in the study of revolution. Some of the issues that are here discussed and some of the questions that are raised are still very much alive in various parts of our world today— struggling nationalities, colonialism, constitutionalism versus revolution, immigration and integration, racism, secret societies, confrontations between establishments and rebels, violence, sectarianism, politico-religious relationships, and so forth. The essays, of course, have a particular relevance for any attempt to understand the two parts of Ireland that are separated from each other by an ideological partition into North and South. In the North, "Fenian" is still a term of abuse which is leveled indiscriminately at the Civil Rights people, Catholics, and nationalists. In the South, "Fenian" is a magical combination of letters, and the South today recalls with pride the memory of her Fenian dead.

Despite the existence of a considerable number of books and articles on the subject, no comprehensive history of Fenianism exists. Much of the history of the movement, indeed, remains unquarried in a wealth of manuscript material that is available in such collections as the police reports in the State Paper Office of Ireland, or in the Public Record Office in London, as well as in the National Archives at Washington and the Public Archives of Canada.

In a sense these essays only scratch the surface of a major area of study. We trust that they offer our readers a freshness of approach and a stimulation. At least they have the merit of combining in one small book reflections of American, British, Canadian, and Irish scholars on the problems of Fenianism. They have the added merit that they open up the consideration of Fenianism to scholars other than historians.

The essay by Seán Ó Súilleabháin, "The Iveragh Fenians in Oral Tradition," introduces us to a world that is as yet virtually untapped by the historian. From the original material that has been collected over the years by the Irish Folklore Commission, the author gives us a glimpse of how the Fenians in a particular area of County Kerry have lived on in the folk memory. These folk traditions pose for the professional historian the challenge of how best to fashion a new methodology that will make the most of a new kind of source. If we would understand the hopes and fears, the attitudes and aspirations of the ordinary people in history, it is clear that the oral tradition is of great significance. The stories here given help to create a genuine historical atmosphere, and they allow us to experience something of the impact made on a revolutionary situation. The County Kerry smith who said: "It isn't the richest man in the world I envy, but the man who sleeps the night without fear", must have millions of unarticulated echoes all over the troubled world of today.

Apart from folklore Irish history also happens to be peculiarly rich in the ballads and poetry of rebellion. The popular expression of Irish nationalism is often to be found in verse—whether it is good verse, or, bad is, for this purpose, beside the point. "Nationalism must be literary", said the Fenian leader, John O'Leary. Certainly every Irish rebellion has produced its crop of versemakers, and Fenianism was no exception. Malcolm Brown in his essay, "Fenianism and Irish Poetry", provides us with some idea of the balladchorus that accompanied the Fenian movement. He argues convincingly that although the early combination of Fenianism with poetry had made a bad start there was to be a luckier combination, leading to Yeats and, one might add, to Joyce. This was so because Fenianism was what Yeats himself described as "the kind of historical crisis which produces literature because it produces passion".

Differences of religion have been intricately interwoven with political developments in Ireland. But to see Catholic and nationalist on one side of an ideological partition and Protestant and unionist on the other does not do justice to the complexities of the real situation. A number of the essays touch upon this topic of politico-religious relations from different points of view. My own essay is devoted specifically to probing the relationship between the Catholic Church and Fenianism. In it I argue that largely because of the clash between Fenian and Prelate a hundred years ago, "Irish" and "Catholic" no longer mean the same thing, and the separation of Church and State in modern Ireland is an essential part of the Fenian legacy.

Norman McCord's essay is a succinct survey of the reaction of ruling class public opinion in Britain to Fenianism. The quotations he has selected from the 1850s gives us some notion of the smugness and complacency of the mid-Victorian establishment's outlook. Fenianism, he shows us, came as a great shock to the ruling classes. In many revolutionary situations the cry, "Conspiracy", is often the first to be uttered by the besieged. The immediate diagnosis of the Fenian phenomenon asserted that the "extravagant and chimerical" idea of an Irish Republic was the product of an external conspiracy emanating from America. The Irish immigrants living in ghettoes in Britain found the problem of integration extremely difficult during the period of the Fenian scare. Racism, with the "Celt" on the receiving end, was also ventilated by the organs of British public opinion. So too, was a sense of injury at Irish ingratitude.

The essay by Robin B. Burns extends the frontiers of Irish, British, and American history to Canada. His essay on D'Arcy departs from some of the traditional views of McGee's development from his revolutionary activities in Ireland in 1848 until his assassination—the only political assassination in Canadian history —by a Fenian twenty years later. Mr. Burns argues that McGee's opposition to Fenianism stemmed less from his involvement in local Canadian politics than from his concern for Ireland's future. In fact McGee's advocacy of a solution for the Irish problem along Canadian lines is a curious anticipation of that which was much later accepted in the Commonwealth experiment after the Anglo-Irish treaty of 1922. The essay also leads us to reflect on the amount of talent there was among the 1848 leaders, and it demonstrates that in order to understand men like McGee in Canada —or Gavan Duffy in Australia, or any of the others for that matter who went abroad—one must examine the Irish background as well as that of the adopted country. The case of Irish rebels who mellowed and became conservative in Canadian, American, and Australian environments suggests a number of interesting questions for further investigation.

Hereward Senior's essay considers the place of the Fenian movement within the Irish Republican tradition, and discusses its similarities and contrasts with other secret societies which Mr. Senior knows so well from his study of Orangeism in Ireland and Britain. He stresses the importance of the Irish-American element which added a new dimension to politics with the growth of an Irish emigrant empire. Michael Hurst's essay is concerned with Fenianism in the context of world history. In the course of this essay he shows that, unlike the collapse that came in the wake of the rebellions of 1798, 1803, and 1848, the military disaster of 1867 did not restrict the impact of Fenianism. The organization remained intact if greatly reduced numerically, and the spirit of Fenianism inspired almost every succeeding drive towards Irish independence and influenced every political, social, or cultural movement of any significance during the half century that followed.

The attentive reader will note different degrees of emphasis and different shades of interpretation in these essays. For example, Mr. Senior does not admit that the connections between Fenianism and the Rising of 1916 were as close as Mr. Hurst implies they were. Mr. Hurst rejects the view which claims that without assistance from the United States the Fenian movement would have fallen apart. Mr. Senior says that had it not been for the Irish-Americans it is doubtful whether a permanent Republican organization could have survived. Again, Mr. McCord questions the efficiency of violence in calling attention to Irish grievances. Mr. Hurst insists that a wide range of legislation was passed at Westminster precisely in the hope of stifling Fenianism.

These and other differences of interpretation should be all to the good, however, and add to the interest of the study of Fenianism.

DONAL McCARTNEY

THE CHURCH AND FENIANISM[1]

DONAL McCARTNEY

THE role of the Catholic Church in the political and social history of Ireland has been undoubtedly great if often only imperfectly understood. The massive ecclesiastical influence may be readily explained by the peculiar course taken by Irish history. From the time of the sixteenth century Reformation Irish political resistance to English rule became closely interwoven with Catholic resistance to the Established Church. And during the ensuing centuries the penal code had the general effect of creating two classes in Irish society. On ones ide of the historical chasm lay the majority, the native Irish peasantry clinging to their religion, poor,i gnorant, dispossessed and leaderless. On the other side were the colonials of the privileged Protestant Ascendancy. In the absence of any sizeable Catholic gentry or middle-class the priest provided local guidance and leadership.

It was the Liberator, Daniel O'Connell, however, who in the early nineteenth century brought the priest into national politics. In the Catholic Association, the first mass-movement of organised democracy in modern Europe, O'Connell made the priests his lieutenants. And ever since the clergy have played a leading part in Irish politics. Archbishops as well as curates were prominent in the Repeal movement, the Tenant League and the Land League. During Parnell's days of glory priests often acted as presiding chairmen over the local meetings of the National League, and after the Parnellite split the priests helped to bring Parnell down.

---

1. The most recent literature on this subject will be found in E. R. Norman, *The Catholic Church and Ireland in the Age of Rebellion 1859-1873* (London, 1965), especially chapter three; and P. J. Corish, *A History of Irish Catholicism*, Vol. V: *Political Problems 1860-78* (Dublin, 1967). Both of these excellent works provide much new material from Roman and Irish episcopal archives. They necessarily emphasise the Roman and Irish episcopal archives. They necessarily emphasise the bishops' side of the case because of the material used. The present article tries briefly to redress the balance somewhat by giving also the Fenian attitude.

In the presence of political giants like O'Connell, and perhaps to a lesser extent Parnell, the clergy were content to act as subalterns. Whenever a vacuum in lay leadership occurred, however, as in the 1850s and 1860s the clergy tended to assume generalship over Irish public opinion. Archbishop, and later Cardinal, Paul Cullen was perhaps the biggest man in Irish affairs between the death of O'Connell in 1847 and the emergence of Parnell in the late 1870s.

Although clerical influence all through the nineteenth century and into the twentieth was powerfully pervasive, it was also complex and never so simple as for example the Unionists took it to be when they declared that Home Rule was Rome Rule. On at least two noteworthy occasions—once in the days of O'Connell during the controversy over the question of granting a Veto to the Crown in the appointment of Catholic bishops, and again in Parnell's time over the Plan of Campaign's withholding of rents—Irish nationalists told Rome in so many words to mind its own spiritual business and leave Irish politics to the Irish. In other words, when ever a question of Anglo-Irish relations was involved the Irish Catholics were not necessarily "Roman". O'Connell said he would as soon take his politics from Constantinople as from Rome. And when he claimed that he loved his religion because it was Irish, it might have been pointed out that he was sailing dangerously close to schism. While, therefore, "Irish" and "Roman" meant separate things, "Irish" and "Catholic" tended more and more to become interchangeable terms as the nineteenth century progressed. It might well have been expected that in the Constitution of a twentieth century independent Ireland Church and State would have been more closely bound together than in fact they are. But as the Irish bishops did not always accept Roman directives in matters political like the Veto, neither did Irish nationalists always accept the bishops' directives. Such separation of Church and State as we have in modern Ireland owes much to the controversy between the Church and the Fenians.

During the eighteenth century the local leadership of the priest was sometimes challenged by the secret agrarian societies. In the mid-nineteenth century the challenge was offered at a national level by the Fenians. And the challenge was given precisely at the moment when Archbishop Cullen was the dominating figure among the hierarchy and was also, allegedly, the grey eminence in political

affairs during the valley period of lay leadership between the pass-
ing of O'Connell and ther ise of Parnell. Sydney Smith once remarked that whoever was the leading ecclesiastic in Ireland would
always be its pope. Bishop Doyle (J.K.L.), Archbishop MacHale
("the Lion of the West"), Archbishop Croke and Archbishop
Walsh were at different times during the nineteenth century minor
popes. None of these made anything like the impact of Dr. Cullen,
an impact which is only beginning to be objectively assessed by the
historians.

Cullen, a great administrator, powerfully influential at Rome
where formerly he had been Rector of the Irish College, was
indeed very much the "Romaniser" of the nineteenth century
Church in Ireland. Under his guidance the Church emerging from
the disintegrating experience of the penal days was brought back
into full discipline with Rome. Contemporaries whispered about the
"Cullenisation" of Ireland. What in effect this meant was that
Cullen drew together the individual bishops and moulded them
into the Irish hierarchy, a formidable weapon geared to serve the
papacy, and strong enough to give politics in Ireland an ecclesiastical slant. Symbolically Roman dress became the fashion among
the priesthood during the Cullen era.

At the very moment when the Irish Church was being more
closely linked with Rome the papacy under Pius IX had
developed a somewhat besieged complex, and this communicated
itself to the Irish hierarchy. The temporal power of the Pope was
under severe attack, while "Liberalism", "Socialism", Freemasonry,
the secret societies were all described as anti-religious and condemned in a number of papal decrees culminating in the Syllabus
of Errors (1864). It had never been more difficult for a Catholic
than in these circumstances to justify his joining a secret, oath-
bound organisation for the purpose of rebellion against the recognised or legitimate government.

From the first stirrings of the Fenian movement in 1858, therefore, the organisation provoked a chorus of episcopal censures led
by Archbishop Cullen of Dublin and Bishop Moriarty of Kerry.
The basis of these censures was firmly stated and constantly reiterated. In the first place, the bishops maintained, a series of papal
bulls, *In eminenti* (1738), *Providas* (1751), *Ecclesiam* (1821), *Quo
Graviora* (1825), had condemned "occult societies". It was, there-

fore, sinful to join such a society, or to try by force to overthrow
the legitimate government. It was wrong to swear blind obedience
to strangers who might not even be men of religion. It was further
stated that the Fenian paper, the *Irish People,* preached socialism
and disrespect for all ecclesiastical authority. And it was claimed
by the bishops that Fenianism only played into the hands of the
enemies of Ireland and of Catholicism; that it was a hopeless
enterprise leading to bloodshed and the ruin of the country. Many
of the clergy used these and similar arguments but Dr. Cullen's
pastoral of 10 October 1865, upon which the above passage has
been based, gives a comprehensive summary of the ecclesiastical
case against the Fenians.[2]

The bishops' stand against Fenianism was inspired not only by
their sense of duty as spiritual guides, but also by their sense of
patriotism (however blunted this may have seemed to extreme
nationalists), and by their genuine concern for the rank-and-file
members of the Brotherhood whom they regarded as being the
dupes of wicked men. And the bishops' position had the support
not only of the constitutional nationalists in O'Connell's tradition,
but also of the ex-'48 men like Smith O'Brien, John Blake Dillon
and John Mitchel. Among the bishops perhaps Moriarty alone was
publicly a Unionist, and he was a Unionist because he held that as
things were in Ireland the people knew no patriotism except hatred
for their rulers. Cullen was too hastily written off by the nationalists
who opposed him as a Castle-bishop. But in his case there is an
abundance of evidence to show that his interest was primarily in
matters like education and not—superficially, at any rate—in
politics at all. Where he did express any political opinions it is
clear enough that his views were moderately nationalist. In the
pastoral already cited in which he denounced Fenianism he also
stated that Ireland ought to be "great, happy and free". And it
is significant that his political hero was O'Connell, the Liberator, if
not also O'Connell the Repealer.

What in practice the bishops' condemnation came to was that
in the confessionals the question was asked whether one had
taken the Fenian oath. Absolution was refused until the penitent

2. For extracts from this pastoral as well as some discussion of Dr.
Cullen's attitude to Fenianism, see P. Mac Suibhne, *Paul Cullen and his
Contemporaries* (Naas, 1961), I, pp. 395-406.

had promised to give up the organisation. The Church's hostility to Fenianism created for many Irishmen a conflict of loyalties : the love of Ireland appeared to be opposed to fidelity to Catholicism. The dilemma was how to be a good Catholic and a Fenian at the same time. For many, who, like John Devoy, took both Fenianism and Catholicism seriously various solutions presented themselves. Devoy has pointed out how in Dr. Cullen's own archdiocese Fenians could go to confession in the Jesuit Church in Gardiner Street, where the priests did not ask the awkward question about the oath.[3] At Christmas and Easter the men of the Fenian circles in Skibbereen in the diocese of Ross crossed over into the diocese of Cloyne where the bishop, Dr. Keane, had not insisted on withholding the sacraments from the Fenians. A young conscientious Fenian who once discussed the matter of the ban with a venerable old priest was told that if he believed it was a virtue to belong to the Brotherhood then the Church had no wish to gratify his vanity by listening to a recitation of his virtues, but if, on the other hand, he believed it was a sin, then he was not wanted in the Brotherhood and the sooner he got out the better.[4] There was many an instance where the interpretation of the episcopal censures by a sympathetic priest left a door open for the man who wanted to reconcile his Fenianism with his religious beliefs.

The Fenians were not solely dependent on the sympathy of a few humble and unnamed priests. It is true, however, that points raised in individual censures were normally refuted in the papers by anonymous letter-writers styling themselves "An Irish Priest", "A Tipperary Priest", "A Country Priest", etc. The most celebrated public protagonist of Fenianism among the clergy was Fr. Lavelle of the parish of Partry in the Archdiocese of Tuam. Lavelle, after a brilliant course in Maynooth, and some time as a professor in the Irish College in Paris, became celebrated as the priest of Partry who outspokenly attacked landlordism and proselytism in his area. In 1861 Dr. Cullen refused to allow a lying-in-state in the Pro-Cathedral for the body of Terence Bellew MacManus, the '48 leader who had died in the U.S.A., because he regarded the whole affair as a Fenian publicity stunt. Fr.

3. John Devoy, *Recollections of an Irish Rebel* (New York, 1929), p. 119.
4. "The Faith of a Fenian", in *Irish Freedom,* Feb. 1911.

Lavelle publicly attacked the Archbishop and the priests of the diocese for their attitude, and travelled to Dublin himself to preach the funeral oration. A few months later, 11 February 1862, Lavelle was back in Dublin's Rotunda lecturing on "The Catholic Doctrine of the Right of Revolution". In his incessant propaganda Lavelle explained that Fenianism was in full accord with the precepts of the Catholic Church, and he insisted that preparation for resistance to a tyrannical government was not only justified but indeed the duty of Irishmen. He ended one of his public statements with a Pauline flourish : "Is this treason? I am then a traitor. Is this disloyal, So am I".[5] On one occasion he argued that the papal bulls against secret societies applied only to those which aimed at the overthrow of Church *and* State, and not to those like the Fenian Brotherhood which aimed only at the overthrow of tyrannical governments. Dr. Cullen, who because of Lavelle's pronouncements in Dublin, felt no doubt somewhat like the lion being bearded in his den, found it necessary to apply to Rome for a ruling in the matter. Lavelle was also Vice-President of the Brotherhood of St. Patrick which was a sort of front-organisation for the Fenians and membership of which was a reserved sin in some of the dioceses.

The bishops, with the exception of Archbishop MacHale of Tuam and Bishop Derry of Clonfert, decided that Lavelle should resign from the Brotherhood and make a public apology. Lavelle, protected by the delaying tactics of his superior, MacHale, was for long able to thwart not only Cullen and the Irish bishops, but even Rome itself. The Lavelle case was, however, regarded as a great scandal by the majority of the Irish ecclesiastics outside of Tuam, for it led to a great deal of wrangling at Rome between the two Archbishops—Cullen, who in 1866 became Ireland's first Cardinal, and MacHale who was dubbed "His Holiness's opposition in Ireland". The issue was also capable of being interpreted as proof that the hierarchy was not united on the question of the "sin" of Fenianism. For this impression MacHale was largely responsible, for he had protected Lavelle. He had also let it be known that he subscribed to the *Irishman,* the mouthpiece of the Brotherhood of St. Patrick which was condemned by name by the

5. Norman, *op. cit.,* p. 112.

bishops. He also donated autographed portraits of himself to the Fenian Fair in Chicago which had been prohibited by Bishop Duggan. And he assisted at High Mass for the Manchester Martyrs when Cullen believed that the real object of these High Masses was to promote Fenianism. There is some evidence to suggest that privately MacHale may not have approved of Fenianism, but he was not going to be bested by Cullen. His stand in the matter, however, had the effect of countering some of the force of the condemnation by the other bishops, and, of course, it made very useful material for the Fenian propagandists.

Although the replies from Rome to Cullen's queries implied that Fenianism came under the ban of papal legislation about secret societies, nevertheless Fenianism was not condemned by name from Rome until January 1870—three years after the Fenian Rising. This, too, allowed Fenian propagandists during the 1860s to argue that their society was not in any way affected by Rome's legislation. Sympathy from individual priests here and there, the silence of some others, the arguments of Lavelle, the apparent goodwill of Archbishop MacHale, and the slowness of Rome in condemning Fenianism by name left many a Fenian with a clear conscience or at least with reasonable doubt. Many others felt that ecclesiastical opinion, whether favourable to Fenianism or not, was altogether irrelevant. Some who believed that they could not serve two masters chose Fenianism and dropped away from the practice of their religion. Others held simply that the Churchmen were acting *ultra vires* by interfering in a political question.

Stephens may have been married in a Catholic Church, but he was never the man to have any personal worries about what ministers of religion had to say to his unorthodox views. Luby was a Protestant, while O'Leary had given up the practice of Catholicism, and both simply regarded the bishops as being no more competent to pronounce on matters political than any other men. The official Fenian reply to clerical critics was usually left to the sincere Catholic, Charles Kickham.

Perhaps the most constantly reiterated message of the *Irish People* during its two years of existence was that of "no priests in politics". It was a grand theme which Kickham made peculiarly his own. In his articles on this topic Kickham maintained that while one could take as much religion as one liked from the priests they were very bad guides to follow in politics. He wrote : "We never uttered a word against the priests as ministers of religion. But we challenged and do challenge their right to dictate to the people in politics".[6] Kickham explained the origins of clerical influence in Irish politics in the following words :[7]

> The Irish priest assumes an authority over his flock which the clergy of other Catholic countries never dream of assuming. Yet this is not to be wondered at. The history of Ireland explains it. The fiendish tyranny of England ground our people down to the condition of ignorant slaves. In this state of compulsory ignorance and serfdom the people naturally looked for guidance to the only educated class that cared for or sympathised with them. But times are changed. The people are now comparatively educated, and demand the right possessed by the people of other Catholic countries of acting according to the dictates of their own judgment in all worldly concerns.

Kickham also claimed that recent Irish history had well illustrated just how fallible priests were. Priests and bishops had been found ready to serve the enemies of their country in 1798 and in 1848. Irish Catholic bishops were "the accomplices of Castlereagh in the murder of their country" by the Act of Union.[8] Their attitude to Young Ireland, their association with the infamous Sadlier and Keogh, their part in the Tenant League fiasco, and their divisions among themselves should warn the people from bowing before clerical dictation in political matters.

The spirit in which the Fenian leaders met the challenge of episcopal censure was also well expressed by Kickham. "We saw from the first", he wrote, "that ecclesiastical authority in temporal affairs should be shivered to atoms before we could advance a single step towards the liberation of our suffering country".[9] Priests, he maintained, were especially unsuited to any form of political leadership. They came straight from a seminary without any experience

6. *Irish People*, 21 May 1864.
7. *Irish People*, 9 April 1864.
8. *Irish People*, 7 May 1864.
9. *Irish People*, 21 May 1864.

of the world.[10] Even the most patriotic of them could not be trusted with leadership for they were not free agents.[11] At a moment's notice, as in the case of the '48 priests and the Tenant Right priests, they would have to accept the ruling of ecclesiastical superiors, and desert the people who had followed their lead leaving them distracted, bewildered and disheartened. It was, therefore, bad for both priests and people that the clergy should get involved and try to lead in matters which were not spiritual. "Sincere and enlightened Catholics justly apprehend great danger from this jumbling together of religion and politics".[12]

The issue between the clergy and the Fenians was one of political morality. It was largely a question of where politics began and the jurisdiction of the Church ended. The controversy appeared to have many of the ingredients needed for the eruption in Ireland of an anti-clericalism somewhat similar to that of contemporary Europe. A *Kulturkampf* of sorts might very well have developed in Ireland, and the signs of the trouble were numerous enough. Dr. Cullen and Dr. Moriarty certainly regarded the Fenian leaders as men who were opposed to the Church and to religion, as men who were the admirers and Irish equivalents of Mazzini, Garibaldi, the Carbonari, the Freemasons and the international socialists. In Bishop Moriarty's famous sermon following the premature rising in Kerry they were described as "designing villains who have been entrapping innocent youth", "criminals", "swindlers" who had "God's heaviest curse, his withering, blasting, blighting curse" upon them, and for whose punishment "eternity is not long enough, nor hell hot enough".[13] In his pastoral, dated 10 October 1865, Dr. Cullen described Fenianism as "a compound of folly and wickedness wearing the mask of patriotism", "the work of a few fanatics and knaves". He asked, "Are they men of religion?" And he suggested the answer in another question : "As needy and desperate adventurers" would they not "introduce despotism and a system of confiscation and the spoilation of all property, public and private?" He continued, "They are said to have proposed nothing less than to destroy the faith of our people

10. *Irish People,* 4 June 1864.
11. *Irish People,* 27 Feb. 1864.
12. *Irish People,* 9 April 1864.
13. *Freeman's Journal,* 10 March 1867.

by circulating works like those of the impious Voltaire, to preach up socialism, to seize on the property of those who have any". Their paper, the *Irish People,* was "a vehicle of scandal" which "circulated in its columns most pernicious and poisonous maxims". The pastoral continued, "Fortunately they had not the wit nor the talents of Voltaire, but according to appearances they did not yield to him in anxiety to do mischief and in malice". The same pastoral lumped together "Fenians, infidels and revolutionists" as "wicked and designing men".

The *Irish People,* on the other hand, in its replies to the clerical critics of Fenianism, also employed strong language. Dr. Cullen would be disappointed, it claimed, if he expected to frighten the people with "hackneyed calumnies",[14] and when bishops and priests "are doing the work of the enemy, we believe it is our duty to tell the people that bishops and priests may be bad politicians and worse Irishmen".[15] The paper candidly admitted that the Fenians contemplated a warfare in which many things would be destroyed—"probably men, women and children would take the place of flocks and herds upon some extensive grass farms with which Dr. Cullen is acquainted".[16]

In the heat of controversy grave misunderstandings arose on both sides. Dr. Cullen was far from being the enemy of his country that the Fenians suggested, and the unworthy implications that he opposed Fenianism because of his concern for his grazier relations, however clever as political tactics, was nevertheless a serious distortion of his true position. On the other hand, while individual Fenians like "Pagan" O'Leary (not to be confused with John) held eccentric religious views, it was no part of official Fenianism to propagate Voltaire's ideas or to attack religion. And Dr. Cullen in circulating in a pastoral what was only being rumoured about the intentions of the Fenians, when the files of the *Irish People* were available to him, was merely employing the same sort of clever but distorted arguments against them which they had used against him.

In taking up the formidable challenge of the hierarchy Kickham and his friends avoided discussing points of theology, morality or

14. *Irish People,* 7 May 1864.
15. *Irish People,* 16 Sept. 1865.
16. *Irish People,* 7 May 1864.

doctrine and deftly shifted the emphasis on to politics. The very motto of Kickham's whole campaign, "no priests in politics", was a signpost to the ground upon which he chose to fight. The more wild and frantic became the pulpit denunciations of the Fenians the easier was it for Kickham and his informants all over the country to select obvious weaknesses and exaggerations in the sermons and use them for Fenian propaganda. Kickham who had a facility in this kind of controversy also had the knack of quoting the priests against the priests as for example when he quoted the seventeenth century scholar, Fr. Luke Wadding : "Time was when we had wooden chalices and golden priests but now we have golden chalices and wooden priests". It must, indeed, have seemed to many of the readers of the *Irish People* that Kickham was more than a match for the "clerical calumniators". His arguments were simple, homely, intelligible and effective. They made sense to the rank-and-file of the Brotherhood. And clearly Kickham's arguments left an impact on the nationalist movement of the future.

Over forty years later in the I.R.B. paper, *Irish Freedom,* an old member of the Brotherhood outlined the "Faith of a Fenian" for the next generation of rebels.[17] In these articles he explained the standt aken by many of his colleagues on the question of the Church and Fenianism. His case was that the greatest of theologians taught that there was nothing morally wrong with the action of a man who after calm reflection was convinced that what he was doing was right. The onus lay on the Church to convince patriotic Irishmen that it was sinful to band together to free their country. He could see nothing reprehensible in an oath taken as an act of devotion to high principles. The Church imposed its own binding vows, but none of these, he submitted with all reverence, was ever taken with higher or nobler motives than those which influenced the Fenians—"Greater love than this no man hath than that a man lay down his life for his friends". The Vatican condemnation of Fenianism, he maintained, had been obtained by English diplomatic influence; and the bishops had been mistaken in classifying Fenianism with those secret societies which had been organised for selfish purposes. If Fenianism did weaken the hold

17. "The Faith of a Fenian", in *Irish Freedom,* Feb. 1911.

of the Church on some men then it was the clergy and not the Fenians who were to blame, for who had first made it a sin to love one's country?

In this statement, and in many similar pronouncements in the *Irish People* and elsewhere, one can see how for many Fenians patriotism had become one of the greatest of the virtues, and long before the days of Pearse the language of religion was already patriotism. Indeed, Pearse almost certainly would have been influenced by such articles as "The Faith of a Fenian" in *Irish Freedom*, in which there were references to the "Founder of Christianity", and to noble motives, and which advised the young Gael not to sit too long by the roadside reading even a Gaelic book. He should rather prepare himself like the Fenians for action and self-sacrifice. Peter O'Neill Crowley, the Fenian hero of the fight in Kilclooney Wood was in ways a striking prototype of Pearse and his companions. Crowley was a respectable unmarried farmer of thirty-five. He was a deeply religious man who was said to have taken a vow of celibacy, and was widely respected in his neighbourhood in Co. Cork. The priest who attended him when he had been mortally wounded has left a report of his dying words : "Father, I have two loves in my heart—one for my religion, the other for my country. I am dying today for fatherland. I could die as cheerfully for the faith".[18]

The religious fervour and the obvious sincerity of Fenian patriotism had their effect. The widespread sympathy and the great demonstrations in connection with the Manchester Martyrs, the massive appeal of the Fenian Amnesty Association and the welcoming home parties for the released prisoners—in all of which priests took an active part—helped to heal the threatened break between Irish nationalism and the Catholic Church. And in this connection, also, the books of two very popular priest-authors played an important, if as yet unrecognised, role. Canon Sheehan especially in such books as *The Graves of Kilmorna,* and an t-Athair Peadar

---

18. Devoy, *op. cit.,* p. 216. For O'Neill Crowley see also Íde Ní Choindealbháin, "Fenians of Kilclooney Wood", in *Journal of the Cork Historical and Archaeological Society,* xlix, no. 170, part 2, 1944, pp. 128-34. A description of Crowley's funeral procession through Fermoy is given in Canon Sheehan's essay "The Moonlight of Memory". The death of O'Neill Crowley inspired his last romance *The Graves of Kilmorna.*

in *Mo Sgéal Féin,* elaborated on the split between the higher and the lower clergy, and between the parish priests and the curates on the question of the Fenians, and the sympathy of the priest-authors was evidently with the Fenians and the younger priests.

After the failure of the Fenian Rising the priests, as if determined to prove their patriotism which had been called into question by the Fenians, got deeply involved in the Land League and the Home Rule agitations. In his *Recollections* in the 1890s John O'Leary remarking on this fact said that it was not the fault of the Fenians if the priests were again prominent in politics. "We meant to kill clerical dictation, and we did kill it. If it has come to life again ina nother generation, the fault is not ours".[19] But in a sense O'Leary was wrong, for it was because of Fenianism that the priests were only too anxious to show their patriotism. And so it was that the priest during Parnell's time was back in politics with a vengeance—if indeed he had ever left.

The Fenian episode, however, had cleared the air somewhat. No longer would clerical denunciation unduly worry extreme or physical force nationalists. Kickham's prophecy was in large part fulfilled. He had concluded in the last number of the *Irish People* before its suppression by the government with the words :

> After all, the war we have been forced to wage against ecclesiastical dictation in politics has done some good. The people are now so used to denunciation there is no room to fear they will be frightened by it when the time has come for the final struggle. This is something to be thankful for.[20]

The bishops were not so vociferous in condemning 1916 as they had been in condemning the Fenians. Seven bishops denounced the 1916 Rising but twenty-two remained silent as if to illustrate the wisdom of the dictum of an early Christian writer : "The more a bishop keeps silence, the more let him be respected". The then Archbishop of Dublin, Dr. Walsh, had perhaps remembered Archbishop Cullen's unhappy quarrel with the Fenians, and publicly maintained a dignified and ominous silence. The silence of the bishops turned in some instances to approbation of the young men who were hitting back during the War of Independence. And

19. John O'Leary, *Recollections of Fenians and Fenianism* (London, 1896), ii, p. 53.
20. *Irish People,* 16 Sept. 1865.

the excommunicated republicans of the Civil War could always recall that the bishops had once condemned the Fenians also.

One outcome of the clash between the Fenians and the Church was that the sectarianism which had done so much to disfigure Irish history in the past was rendered largely irrelevant. In the eighteenth century Irish Protestants had persecuted Irish Catholics. In the nineteenth century the situation threatened to become in time reversed, for with the achievements of O'Connell Irish Catholic democracy became aware for the first time of its great strength. The Church emerging from the catacombs of the preceding centuries, like new rich everywhere was understandably proud of its triumphs and somewhat arrogant in its attitudes. Dr. Cullen was the personification of its new spirit. The 1850s which was the period of the Catholic Defence Association and of the "Pope's Brass Band" saw the writing on the wall that sectariansim in the future was more likely to be at the expense of Irish Protestants than Catholics. And Young Irelanders like John Kells Ingram in Trinity College were frightened off the national cause. Fenianism, however, intervened in the 1860s and helped to make sectarianism irrelevant, both by recovering and propagating the non-sectarian ideas of the United Irishmen and the Young Irelanders, and by diverting ecclesiastical fire away from Orangemen, proselytisers, Trinity College and "Godless colleges", and drawing it instead upon themselves.

Another by-product of the clash was that the more clearly the Fenian tradition and Fenian sympathies seemed to lie behind later Irish leaders the more ready were the bishops to listen to them, or to put this perhaps in a more accurate way, the slower were the bishops to condemn them. One suspects that some of Parnell's or De Valera's strength during their periods of power owed not a little to this fact.

A head-on clash between Irish nationalism and the Catholic Church had been averted, for in the end neither side had really wanted to fight the other. In the process, however, each had learned to regard the other with a healthy respect. And largely because of the Fenian episode "Catholic" and "Irish" no longer necessarily meant the same thing. One of the propositions condemned in the Syllabus of Errors of Pius IX was the doctrine that Church and State should be separated. If in a modern Ireland Church and

State have been separated to an extent undreamed of by Pius IX part of the explanation is to be found in Fenianism. For, in their own often inarticulate and non-philosophical way the Fenians had insisted on separating the state which they sought to overthrow from the Church to which the majority of them belonged. And this, as truly as their gospel of physical force or their republicanism, was to be an essential part of the Fenian heritage.

THE IVERAGH FENIANS IN ORAL TRADITION

SEÁN Ó SÚILLEABHÁIN

THE peninsula of Iveragh in South Kerry was the scene of a good deal of Fenian activity prior to 1867, and when word of the post-ponement of the rising had not reached them by the 12th February, of that year, the members of the organisation there took the field. The main events of the next few days were concerned with the raid on the Coastguard Station at Kells, to the east of Caherciveen, the shooting of a policeman at Esk near Glenbeigh, the march towards Killarney, the hiding in Coill na dTóime (Tomies Wood) near that town, the final withdrawal towards their homes, and the search, pursuit, arrest and trial, followed by transportation, of several of those who took part. It was all over in a few days, save for the aftermath when Government troops and police were again in control.

Local traditions of the rising in Iveragh, which I have en-deavoured to summarise in this article, have been taken from manuscripts in the archives of the Irish Folklore Commission. They were all recorded in the Irish language in that barony by Tadhg Ó Murchadha, one of the fulltime collectors of the Commission, during the years 1936-52. Some of the forty or so informants had actually seen the Fenians; others had got their information from people who had witnessed the occurrences described.

The leader of the Iveragh Fenians was J. J. O'Connor, who had emigrated from Valentiat o the United States as a youth, had been wounded in the American Civil War, and had returned to Caher-civeen towards the end of 1865. He started to recruit local young men as members of the Fenians, aided by Mortimer Moriarty, who had also returned home after the American Civil War. The names of scores of Fenians occur in the local oral accounts, among them young Connolly (son of the sergeant of police in Caher-civeen), John Goulden, Tom Griffin, Conway (who wounded the policeman), Corney O'Brien and Sheehan, head of the Killarney men.

While recruiting and drilling were going on in 1866, one account says that "all the people around used to be afraid of the Fenians—

that they might take any moneyt hey had".[1] Again, "some of the young lads around here used to take to the hills on the run, in fear of the Fenians coming and forcing them to join".[2] Still, the general attitude appears to have been one of loyalty, although there is reference to one woman who got a bounty for informing on the Fenians[3] and to somebody whose ears were cut off in punishment for giving information to the police.[4] The manuscripts have many accounts of the ways in which people succoured and sheltered the Fenians on the run when the rising was over.

Drilling in preparation for the rising took place at night, generally on strands at low water, both in the island of Valentia, and in neighbouring mainland areas (Dromad, Filemore, Eochair Mong, An Tráigh Bhán, near Caherdaniel, and elsewhere). The places chosen for drilling were, we are told, *cúl le faobhar* (remote).[5] Still, they had to be on the alert : Jerh. Kelly, an agent of the landlord, Leahy of Caherdaniel, saved the Fenians who were drilling on the strand by riding on horseback to warn them of the approaching police.[6] So too, Dr. Barry sent word from Caherciveen to Paddy Daly, who was head of the Dromad Fenians, that a raid was imminent; Barry was fond of hunting, as was Daly, and they often met; Daly had barely hidden a hundred guns and revolvers in the mountain when the raid took place—the cache was never since found, although it has often been searched for.[7] Seán Ó Luasa of Filemore aged 82 in 1942, told how he, when nine years old, had often seen Corney O'Brien, Jack Goulden and Tom Griffin "playing marbles behind the old house each day in summer"[8]—to pass the time, presumably, until they moved on.

Organisation and drilling went on secretly. Mícheál Conraoi of Gleesk, Glenbeigh, told in 1944 : "My mother came to this townland in 1866. She wasn't long here when a fine handsome man came in to her one day. She was baking a yellow-meal cake on the griddle, and he got a desire for it. She gave him some of it, and he ate it. He was an O'Brien from Cork, a captain of the Fenians; my

In these footnotes, the number of the Irish Folklore Commission manuscript volume, followed by the relevant pages, is given in each case.

1. 146:515-6.
2. 1312:502.
3. 1312:502.
4. 964:224-9.
5. 1006:534.
6. 146:512-6.
7. 372:224-4.
8. 797:459-60.

father knew him. He came in often after that; he used to be writing letters and things. A year later they rose out. They knew when they came to Kells that they were sold; they saw no bonfires there—the bonfire was their signal".[9]

Pádraig Mac Gearailt remembered how his father took him, at the age of nine, to Caherciveen to get a pair of shoes made for him. He saw Fenians coming down the street from the direction of Killarney and entering both the National and Munster banks. "But they took no money, whatever happened". Next day, Pádraig heard at his home that Muiris 'ac Séamuis Uí Chonaill, with two or three hundred soldiers, were searching the woods around Glenbeigh for the Fenians. Muiris finally reached the house of Diarmán Ó Conchobhair in Glencar—this Diarmán was a great seanchaí and storyteller, and Muiris, who was a great fowler, often called to hear his tales. Diarmán had seven Fenians eating a meal in his house when Muiris and the soldiers came into the yard. Muiris entered and asked were there any Fenians about—the seven had escaped to the room below the kitchen. Diarmán said that there weren't; he wouldn't allow them next or near his house, he said. "We were told that they were here", said Muiris, "and we must take a look". He had his hand on the latch of the room-door, when Diarmán started to tell him a new story, and so interested did Muiris become that he never raised the latch. "It was lucky for Muiris that he didn't; the Fenians would shoot him and be shot by the soldiers themselves". When the story was finished, Diarmán told him to search around Lickeen, where, he had heard, the people were feeding the Fenians. "Three of the men in the room were named Ó Cuirc, and one of them was an O'Brien, a brother of the parish priest of Prior."[10]

On Shrove Tuesday O'Connor sent Mortimer Moriarty on the mailcar to Killarney with a letter for Sheehan, head of the Fenians there, promising help in the rising. Moriarty and Sheehan were both arrested that day, as the Killarney police had got word from Caherciveen about their activities. That night, a Shrove Tuesday dance,t he last until the end of Lent, was being held in Caherciveen, when the dancers were told to leave the hall long before the usual time. In the street they found about thirty Fenians on

9. 929:558-9.   10. 149:448-53.

parade, with guns and pikes. They did not attack the barrack in the town as a gunboat in the harbour would have shelled them. They marched to Barry's Big House, "over the water" (a district beside the town), and took some guns from there. The Valentia men had not joined them, through some mistake, so they set out eastwards to meet the Filemore men at Kells Coastguard Station. Two of the coastguards were away, one was in bed, and the fourth (Tom Pierce) was on guard with a rifle nearby. A shot was fired and Pierce ran, abandoning his rifle. Five rifles, four pistols and a box of powder were taken from the watch-house. The wife of one of the guards recognised a few of the Fenians, including Goulden, and later gave evidence against him[11]—her name was Lizzie Goggin, later pilloried in an Irish song, one verse of which was :

Cuirfimíd Goggin sa Sceilg,
Cuirfeam ar bord an rí í,
Curifeam anonn thar farraige í,
Féachaint an ndéanfaí díon di.[12]

The raiders then called at the house of Dr. Barry, who lived nearby, and took his horse for their leader, O'Connor, who was lame and badly able to walk. The seventy Fenians then set out for the long march eastwards to Killarney. At Esk, where the idle railway tunnels now are, above the sea, they met a horseman. This was a Constabe Duggan, who had been despatched from Killorglin, on the orders of the Killarney police (who had earlier in the day arrested Moriarty and Sheehan—the Caherciveen men were not aware of this yet). Duggan was on his way to Caherciveen to warn the police there and carried a list of names of the prominent local Fenians. He refused to halt when challenged and Conway fired a shot, which injured him in the thigh. He fell from the horse and was taken by the Fenians into the little house of Diarmaid a' Bhuana Moriarty (Diairmín na hEisce), below the road.[13] He said that he was a Catholic and asked for a priest and doctor.[14] O'Connor examined his wound and said he had often

11. 1312:499-500.
12. 928:242-3.
13. 1312:500-1.
14. 961:561-4.

seen worse in the American war. Fr. Maginn of Glenbeigh and Dr. Spotswood were sent for (the Fenians were later commended for this). Duggan lived, and Diarmaid Moriarty later got a bounty which enabled him to build a better house, on the gablewall of which was a stone with the name Duggan inscribed on it.[15] One narrator, Mícheál Ó Braonáin, remembered his father telling how he had seen the wounded Duggan sitting near the fire in a house near Glenbeigh a fortnight later; "he was as white as the wall".[16] A list of names of Fenians, "and the names of a lot that weren't in the Fenians at all', was found on Duggan between the saddlecloth, together with news of the arrests in Killarney.[17]

The atmosphere of the following day is well described by Máire Ní Mhurchadha, who was five or six years old at that time. "The day after the raid on Kells, my grandmother was sick in the room; my father was reading out of a book for two or three fellows in the kitchen—a book was worth a lot at the time. There was a knock at the door, and a young man came in, dressed in shepherd plaid, white and black; he called out one of the fellows and was whispering to him; that fellow came back and started whispering to the others : '*Beidh scéal nua amáireach againn*'. The Coastguard Station at Kells had just been raided. Next morning, every person that met anyone else was whispering, and we didn't know in the world what they were saying."[18]

The Fenians got some food in the morning at O'Shea's inn at Glenbeigh, and O'Connor paid for it in cash. Fr. Maginn gave the Fenians his blessing, although his brother, who was parish priest in Valentia, was strongly opposed to the Fenians. They then continued on their way to the east towards Killarney (it is hard to understand why, as they now knew that the rising had not taken place elsewhere). Still, on they went; O'Connor sent Dr. Barry's horse home to him and rode Duggan's mount. They went through Kilcoolaght, bypassing Killorglin, and finally reached Coill na dTóime, southwest of Killarney.

Panic had seized the police and gentry of that town (soldiers had not yet arrived); the more wealthy persons had sent their money and valuables to the hotel, which was sandbagged for

15. 146:512-6. 17. 777:556.
16. 929:351-2. 18. 531:175-8.

protection. "'Twas thought the Fenians were going to rob the bank in Killarney," Mícheál Ó Conchobhair of Listry, aged 94 in 1940, remembered; "the bankers carried every shilling of money that was in it up to the Railway Hotel and put sandbags outside the windows to save it."[19]

The Fenians had no such plans, however. They knew that their best plan was to hide in the woods around Tomies and Beaufort for a day or two and then set off for home again. They had no food and had to depend on the generosity of the people around. Eoghan Ó Súilleabháin (aged 84 in 1940) remarked that the people near Killarney were afraid of the Fenians; "they knew nothing about them, and were afraid they would kill everybody".[20] Some Fenians called to the house of Neddy O'Real, near where Gleann Chotáin School is now; they were looking for food; they drank all the milk he had (he had only a few cows) and ate all the butter, but they paid him by pushing money under the door.[21] "Two or three others called to the house of a man near Coill na dTóime. The man told them he had no food *beirbhthe* (cooked) but it wouldn't take him long. He went out for a *cliabh* of turf to put down a fire; the Fenians took off their shoes and were near the fire when word came that the soldiers were coming. They ran out as fast as they could to join the rest, and spent the day till evening trying to make their way out of the woods towards the mountain." "They blamed their leader for the plight they were in," Mícheál Ó Braonáin of Prior said. " 'I'm deeper in it than ye are,' the leader retorted, 'and ye can shoot me, if ye wish—I'd rather ye would do so than anyone else'."[22] Pádraig Ó Donnchadha of Beaufort (aged 83 in 1940) remembered the Fenians well. "They passed through the Black Valley and called to my father's house, about thirty of them. They ate cold potatoes and meat and cabbage. Each of them had a gun. The redcoat soldiers came looking for them the next day but didn't find them. The Fenians were ahide in the hills and they could have killed the soldiers, who were hungry and falling here and there, if they wished. The soldiers had justices and gentry with them to order them to fire if they saw the Fenians."[23]

19. 715:559.
20. 715:530-6.
21. 715:530-6.

22. 961:561-4.
23. 716:169-71.

Eoghan Ó Súilleabháin, already quoted, told how he was pulling weeds in a potato-garden at Meanus when he heard people running east and west on the road. The soldiers were coming, they said. "Men who had horses and cars on the road untackled them and tied the horses at the roadside and ran. A half-mile of the road was full of soldiers riding huge horses with white foreheads, three abreast. They marched on to Caherciveen, looking for the Fenians, but did no harm. O'Connor wanted the Fenians to ambush them at Gabhal an Phocáin; if they did, they would kill them all, but instead they went into Coill na dTóime and hid there."[24]

The atmosphere of those disturbed days may be discerned in the following anecdotes. Mícheál Ó Braonáin's father in Prior, with a neighbour, were about to set out for Killorglin for a load of oats; on hearing that the Fenians were rising, they put back their journey until a fortnight later. A smith in Caherciveen was quoted by Ó Braonáin as saying : "It isn't the richest man in the world I envy, but the man who sleeps the night without fear".[25] Pádraig Óg Liath Ó Súilleabháin, aged 84 in 1945, told how Tadhg Ó Súilleabháin of Cloghanakeen had a neighbour named Liam Ó Murchadha. This neighbour was so worried about his son who was taking part in the raid on Kells Coastguard Station that night that Tadhg found him with a razor in his hand, about to commit suicide. Two hours later, news came that none of the Fenians there had been arrested.[26] Mrs. Nora Fenton, aged 89 in 1944, told how, as a girl of twelve, she was sent by her parents for messages to Caherciveen. When she went into Connor an tSalainn's shop for salt, which was manufactured there, she heard J. J. O'Connor's sister wailing loudly that her brother was being sought for by the soldiers. On her way home with the messages, she saw three Fenians coming down the hillside from Rinnard; "they were probably Valentia men making their way back home".[27] Pádraig Mac Gearailt, aged 77 in 1935, of Cill an Ghoirtín, described how his father, Myles, used to sell meal and flour, which he used to obtain at Latchford's store in Caherciveen before the rising. Some of the wealthy people in the town told him that he was foolish to spend his money on meal and flour (much of which he gave free to the poor); he should keep his money, as

24. 715:530-6.
25. 961:561-4.
26. 963:271-5.
27. 961:492-3.

no one knew what lay ahead. He replied that they were still more foolish to have their money in the National Bank, which the Fenians might raid at any time (they did raid it, as we have seen, but took no money).[28]

As might be expected, stories about the searches made by soldiers and police for the Fenians after the rising, as well as the narrow escapes of some of them, form a large corpus within the oral traditions of the period. One of the Dodds family of Killorglin was one night hiding at Sheehan's house in Dromad when word came that the "peelers" were nearby. Domhnall Ó Súilleabháin, a comrade of Dodds, ran out into the yard where his stallion was tethered; Dodds jumped up behind him on the animal's back, and both of them reached Com a' Sathairn safely.[29] Séamus Raol of Binn Bhán was high in the Fenians (his nickname was Major O'Reilly); after the rising, he returned home but was spied on and reported. When the "peelers" came to search his house one night, he rushed to the room and hid himself between the bed and the wall; one of the searchers noticed him but did not pretent anything. The sergeant in charge carried out a further search, with the light of a candle, found Raol and arrested him. He was transported to Australia and returned home later, but said he was sorry he had not stayed there.[30] J. J. O'Connor was hiding in the house of Diarmaid na Bó in Glencar. He was spied on, and Muiris 'ac Séamuis Uí Chonaill arrived one night, with a band of soldiers, to arrest him. When Diarmaid opened the door for them, he fell in a faint, thinking he would be hanged for sheltering a Fenian. His wife was asked what was wrong with her husband and she replied that he had been subject to fits like that as long as she had known him. O'Connor heard the voices in the kitchen and, when the soldiers searched the loft where he was, he hid himself under a pile of birch brooms and escaped detection.[31]

A Palatine who lived at Aghatubrid was a very charitable man and would refuse food or shelter to nobody who came to his house. "Two Fenians, on the run, trusted him and came to his house one night. They were seen going there and were reported to the police. When they came to search the house, the Palatine denied that any Fenians had been there. 'Ye know well it isn't to

28. 146:111-3.
29. 797:459-60.
30. 927:186-9.
31. 1226:99-100.

the likes of me they would come,' he said to the sergeant. The police left without searching, and the two Fenians set off to the hill again next day, *mo ghraidhn iad!*"[32] Another man in Dromad had a namesake of his from Valentia, a Fenian, hiding in his house one night. When the police came, the man of the house opened the door, and the Fenian went into bed with the woman of the house. The police, thinking that the man in the bed belonged to the house and that the man who had opened the door for them was the Fenian, arrested the latter and took him off to the barracks. To make matters worse for the arrested man a roguish neighbour of his, on being asked to identify the prisoner, denied that he knew him at all. He was released later, however; in the meantime, the Fenian made off across the mountains to Co. Cork and got a boat there which took him to America.[33]

Mrs. Shea of Lohar often told Seán Sigerson, aged 65 in 1938, how two Fenians came to her house one night. "They were two fine, decent fellows, well-dressed and seemingly of good stock. There was no sign of hunger on them. Both had guns. One of them in turn stretched himself out on the *raca* (seat) in the kitchen to doze, while the other stood on guard outside. They changed places a few times during the night and left when the day dawned. They had their own food with them." The same informant said that Fr. Donncha Ó Súilleabháin, P.P., of Caherdaniel, kept some Fenians in his house. He was spied on, and the "peelers" came to search. The priest met them at the door and asked who had sent them; whatever answer they gave, he ordered them to leave and not to come again until he sent for them. A boat from Ráth took the Fenians across Kenmare Bay to Béara at the dawn next morning.[34] Pádraig Ó Carúin, aged 66 in 1941, said: "An old woman whom I knew told me that five of the Fenians came in to her in the middle of the night (at Cnoc Rua, in Barra na Haoine). They were exhausted, and everys titcho f their clothes was torn from the heath and furze on the hills. She gave them food, and they asked her would she wash their socks—that they hadn't taken them off for a month. She said that she would. She herself had to remove the socks from their feet, and all the skin under the socks came away when she pulled them off. She kept the five for a fortnight.

32. 997:552-4.   34. 667:78-80.
33. 995:440-2

She had goats' *blonag* (lard) and unsalted butter which she rubbed on each day until their feet had healed. They left her then and went somewhere else until things cooled down."[35]

A man from Dromad was arrested when returning to Caherciveen for a parcel which he had forgotten there. He admitted to the soldiers that he was a Fenian, was taken first to Caherciveen barracks and next day to Killarney. He spent a month in jail (said Seán Ó Murchadha, aged 72 in 1939) before being tried. Fr. O'Connor, who was a curate in Dromad, went to the courtroom in Killarney to plead for him. "How long have you known this man?" asked the judge. "'Tis longer than you know this soldier who is giving evidence against him; you never laid eyes on him until this morning," said the priest. The man was sent to Dublin and was a year in jail.[36] Mícheál Ó Móráin of Dromad, who was four years old at the time of the rising, told how a local "peeler" who was on holidays in his married brother's house there overheard, while in the room, a local Fenian tell the people of the house that he and some other Fenians were leaving for America next day. The "peeler" took note of the names and told Capt. Ross, who was in charge of the local soldiers. The Fenians were arrested. Capt. Ross promised the "peeler" that he would try to get a job for him in the Bridewell as caretaker. When the letter of thanks and the offer of the job came from Dublin, the "peeler" celebrated his good furtune by drinking in Caherciveen; he lost the letter in the course of the carousing, and it was found by Morty Kelly, who was a friend of the Fenians. The "peeler" searched the town for the letter next day, and when he failed to find it, he disappeared from the district.[37]

Soldiers and police searched everywhere for the Fenian leader, O'Connor, but failed to catch him.[38] Pádraig Ó Súilleabháin of Valentia, aged 65 in 1941, told how O'Connor was at the house of Seán de Búrca in Caherciveen one day. "The police were wild, east and west, searching for him. The lads in the house, and Seán de Búrca too, told him to go ahide. 'I won't,' said O'Connor, 'But I'll bet a pound that I'll go out begging in the street, and I'll beg from nobody but the police.' He went out into the backyard and came back as an old man, small and grey and lame—even

35. 777 : 557-8.   37. 1147 : 203-6.
36. 612 : 19-25.   38. 961 : 494.

the lads inside didn't know him! Out into the street with him then, and he went to every peeler in the street and returned with a fistful of money from them, and they didn't recognise him!"[39] O'Connor finally escaped from Cuan Trae to a ship that took him to America, where he died at an early age soon after.[40]

John Goulden, who had been identified by Lizzie Goggin as having taken part in the Kells raid, made his way to Queenstown where he was arrested with another Fenian and sent to Botany Bay. Released after some time, he made his way to Australia, where he married. A neighbour of his there visited Ireland in the early thirties and called to see Goulden's relatives. He said that Goulden was then dead, but his family were doing well in Australia. Conway, who shot Duggan, came home from America later, Pádraig Ó Carúin said. "He was a fine man, fairly old. He had a house in Caherciveen. When he would walk out after his supper in the evening, the old people used to point him out to the young and say: 'That's the Fenian who shot the peeler at Cnoc Droinge.' It was a cause for great wonder at the time that any man was courageous enough to shoot a peeler".[41]

Michael O'Connor of Listry, aged 94 in 1940, told the following story about some of the men who had been transported: "Jerry Sheehan of Milltown was arrested and spent a long time in jail. He was a clerk in Killarney and was one of the head men of the Fenians. Word came to him that a raid was threatened, and he rushed upstairs and burned all the documents containing names of the Fenians. He was arrested and transported for life along with some others. Members of Parliament began to agitate for their release, and after a number of years all were let go except six who had been soldiers of the Queen. Some carpenters who were doing repairs in the prison spent a lot of money among the warders, and one fine morning when the bell rang for all the prisoners, the six soldiers were missing. A boat followed them but they reached American waters and escaped. Sheehan's brother, who lived near Sir James O'Connell, asked Sir James to sign a petition to let Jerry come home. 'I'll sign it for you, Mick, though he was a Fenian,' said Sir James. 'Ah, he wasn't,' said old Mick. 'He was, Mick,' said Sir James, 'and every child that was born to his

39. 797:413-5.   41. 777:560-1.
40. 146:516.

mother was another.' Jerry was let come home, and he married a widow woman in Killarney."[42]

Mention is made in some accounts of the places in which the Fenians hid their guns when the rising had failed. Pats Rúntach found twelve guns stacked in a cave at Tuairíní, but they fell to pieces, eaten with rust, when he touched them.[43] O'Connor and Conway used visit Tadhg Leary's house at Maoilinn, Mícheál Ó Siochfhradha of Prior, aged 78 in 1947, said : "When the Fenians were broken up, there was a big box of arms in the house, and they and Tadhg took it east into the mountain and buried it there, in Tadhg's land, and it is there ever since."[44] Pádraig Ó Carúin said that the Fenian guns were barrel-loaded with powder and shot and would fire further than the present-day rifles. "They were buried on both sides of the Aoine River, between Bealach Oisín and the Aoine Bridge. They were stuffed into the inches and bogs, and they are still there. I think some of them were found when turf was being cut."[45]

Muiris 'ac Séamuis Uí Chonaill, Chief Constable for Kerry at the time of the rising, was unpopular because of the raids to catch the Fenians. Pádraig Óg Liath Ó Súilleabháin, already mentioned, was in Caherciveen one day, as a child, with his father and mother. "The street was red with soldiers from end to end, with Muiris at their head. I saw a woman bending down in the channel of the street, and she lifted up a dead rat and struck Muiris with it in the chest."[46]

Finally, what is probably an apocryphal anecdote about Dr. Moriarty, Bishop of Kerry, who had strongly condemned those who were behind the Fenian movement. Michael O'Connor of Listry, aged 94 in 1940, told how Bishop Moriarty went into a barber's shop in Mallow later. "He wasn't dressed like a bishop at all, but the barber had a suspicion who he was. When he had half of his face shaved, the barber said 'Is there any chance that you are the Lord Bishop of Kerry?' 'I am not at all,' said the bishop. ' 'Tis well for you that you aren't,' said the barber, 'for I'd cut you throat if I thought you were!' The devil a bit of me but I suppose he'd do it!"[47]

42. 715:559-63.
43. 928:241-2.
44. 1006:533.

45. 777:558-9.
46. 963:271-9.
47. 715:568-9.

THE FENIANS AND PUBLIC OPINION IN GREAT BRITAIN

NORMAN McCORD

THE object of this paper is to discuss the reaction in Great Britain to the activities of the Fenians. In evaluating the role of the Fenians this is not a useless exercise, for it must be obvious enough that in the third quarter of the nineteenth century the best chance for alleviation of Ireland's difficulties still lay with the Parliament of the United Kingdom, and that the persuading or over-awing of that legislature into concession was Ireland's most reasonable hope for beneficial change. Certainly the Fenians contemplated the overthrow of the British ascendancy by force, but the chances of success here were very remote, and in practice the reality of power still rested at Westminster. No attempt is made here to evaluate the place of the Fenians in the history of Irish nationalism, but only to discuss how the predominant element in the United Kingdom reacted to their activities.

"Public opinion" is an essentially vague term, and discussion of it clearly proffers its own difficulties. Obviously in a subject like this there wasn't simply one unified public opinion, but rather a number of public opinions, varying in extent and importance. Fortunately for our purposes we are not dealing with a modern liberal democratic state—despite the fact that the main crisis of Fenianism in Great Britain co-incided with an important stage in the rise of the working classes in Britain—but a society in which political power was still effectively concentrated in a limited group. For practical purposes here the main concern must be how those segments of British society capable of exercising influence on policy reacted to the Fenians, though there are some interesting reactions elsewhere to be considered.

How can one attempt to reconstruct opinion among the influential groups in Great Britain? There are of course a number of very obvious sources to go to : Parliamentary Debates, which after all represent reasonably well the reactions of those actually in power, diaries, speeches, the newspapers, especially *The Times,* which, while not an infallible guide to opinion, clearly was believed to exercise considerable influence, a belief which in itself played some part in moulding opinion. None of these is completely reliable, but in this case their corporate voice may perhaps be trusted, for on the one hand they are in tolerable harmony, and on the other there isn't anything to suggest that in this instance they present a misleading picture of opinion in Great Britain.

In the years just before Fenianism began Irish affairs hardly seemed a topic of pressing urgency in Great Britain. There were those, among British as well as Irish politicians, who continued to urge the United Kingdom Parliament to act more effectively to introduce reforms to Ireland, but they were a small and not very influential minority, many of whom were regarded as somewhat cranky and in any event apart from the reality of contemporary British politics. Much more general was an attitude of complacency, which was scarcely much shaken by the first comparatively mild instances of Fenian activity in Ireland. A debate in the House of Lords in February 1859[1] produced categorical assurances from Irish landowners that recent years had seen an enormous improvement in the situation in Ireland. Viscount Dungannon roundly asserted that :

> ... at no period was Ireland in a greater state of prosperity than it was at the present moment; and he was convinced that this statement would be borne out by all who like himself were connected with Ireland, and were interested in her welfare ...

The Earl of Desart was only slightly less dogmatic :

> ... Any man who had witnessed the condition of Ireland in 1849, and should revisit it after this lapse of ten years would scarcely recognize the country, so much had its condition improved. It was no doubt greatly to be lamented that there should still exist in the country a disposition to shelter from justice the perpetrators of crime, but he believed even that spirit was dying out, and he hoped to see the day when it would cease entirely ...

A year later even the Marquess of Clanricarde declared that Ireland "... now was one of the most tranquil in Europe ..."

1. *Parliamentary Debates*, CLII, 237-7 (Dungannon, Desart); CLVI, 1919 (Clanricarde).

In addition there frequently occurred smug references to the valuable part which wise legislation had played in the process of improvement. The effectiveness of the Encumbered Estates legislation was greatly exaggerated in Great Britain, and was one factor credited by *The Times* on several occasions with the beneficial changes—others being the easing of emigration, and the horrible but necessary removal of surplus population which the Famine had brought.[2] Such complacency could reach strange lengths :[3]

> ... There is literally nothing within the powers of Government which Parliament has not done, or is not ready to do, for her. Nor can we admit that all these efforts have failed. On the contrary there is more real progress than at any earlier period ...

Many references to Ireland stressed her recent orderly behaviour, and it was widely assumed that the sister island was now willing to do her duty in the station to which she had been called.

Fenianism certainly did much to shatter this complacency. Even the comparatively minor outbreaks of the late 1850s focussed attention on Ireland. The reaction to the first manifestations of discontent tended to be one of derision. *The Times* wrote of "very green nationalists" and "this confederation of fools",[4] but the Irish reaction to the first Fenian activities evoked second thoughts. At the beginning of 1859 an editorial in *The Times* once again recited the boons which Britain had conferred on Ireland, and went on to express bitter disappointment at Irish ingratitude :[5]

> ... The return, after so many years intermission, to Riband Societies, to a course of agrarian crime, to treasonable oaths and secret conspiracies, is certainly a bitter disappointment to our bright and sanguine hopes. We had dreamt of another future for Ireland, and can scarcely prevail upon ourselves to awake and look in the face our present disappointments—to admit how deeprooted are the evils with which we have

2. Eg., 4-1-1859.
3. 19-9-1865.
4. 11 and 13-12-1858.
5. 4-1-1859.

striven to contend, and how ill the race in whose destiny
we are so deeply interested profits by the opportunities of
prosperity or the teaching of adversity ... If the Irish cannot
be content with their lot, the fault we are now convinced is
theirs, not ours ...

Yet it is noticeable how quickly attention in Great Britain left
Irish problems and thankfully returned to matters nearer home
when once the pressure of events in Ireland slackened. This is
perhaps readily understandable in the events of the late 1850s, but
it is striking that the same comment can be applied to the sixties
and seventies too. Complacency had certainly returned by October
1863 when *The Times* could reflect happily[6] of Ireland that:

... the country was never in a state of greater tranquillity.
Never, perhaps, since the Union was there such an entire
absence of complaints against the Government ...

Such smugness was to have a very rude awakening in the next
few years. During the recrudescence of Fenian activity from 1865
there was at first little attempt to consider whether there might
be real grievances involved, and rather still the pious hope that
once this little gang of fools and villains was extirpated Ireland
would appreciate the blessings brought by the British connection.
Once again we may take comments by *The Times* in these autumn
months of 1865 as a fair reflection of "mainstream" opinion among
influential groups in Britain.[7]

... Their enterprise may not be the wickedest, but, so far as
we can judge, it is by far the wildest, except, perhaps Smith
O'Brien's, that has yet been planned by Irish agitators. Almost
the only thing we know for certain about them is that the
establishment of an Irish Republic is one of their main objects.
A more extravagant and chimerical idea never entered the
head of an Irishman ... Is there any people under the sun
more unfit for a Republican form of Government than the
Irish? Is there any character so deficient in those political
virtues which are the life of Republics as the Celtic? ... The
truth is that Fenianism has not and could not have sprung
up spontaneously on Irish soil. It is entirely of exotic growth,

6. 23-10-1863.
7. 18-9-1865, 22-9-1865, 27-9-1865, 30-9-1865, 8-11-1865.

an importation from America, and entirely out of harmony
with real Irish sentiment ...

... it does not seem consistent with either reason or pro-
bability that any number of men should have carried so
absurd a project to such a ridiculous reality ...

... The more completely the scheme is revealed, the more
supremely absurd does it appear ... That the whole scheme in
its origin and conception was American rather than Irish is
beyond all doubt ... The very exaggeration of the idea is
transatlantic, and nothing, we suspect, but credulity and folly
has been contributed from native sources ... When Irish
disaffection has dwindled to Fenianism, there is good reason
for supposing that it is dying out altogether, and must be very
near its end ...

A rankling sense of injury at Irish ingratitude can also be detected
in these weeks, although these were not nearly as splenetic as those
of a couple of years later :

... No good administration on the part of the Queen's Government can eradicate at once the animosities which have grown
up during so many generations. The Fenians are the grand-
children of the rebels of 1798, and their youth was passed
amid the harangues of O'Connell and the conspiracies of
Smith O'Brien. When such a population as the Irish have
such memories a Government of angels would not content
them ... All we can recommend is patience, and as much
lenity to these would-be revolutionists as is consistent in keeping them out of mischief for the future ...

... Ireland by being associated with England has obtained a
very much better Government than she would have had, had
she been left to herself ... It was not in the power of
England to force the Irish to trust one another, or to practice
in their own country, at least, that steady and persevering
industry which has raised England to her present position.
Therefore, though extremely well governed, Ireland is not
happy or prosperous ...

Roebuck roundly declared[8] in March 1866 that "... Ireland, if left to herself, would afford such a spectacle of misery as mankind have ever witnessed ..."

These patronising positions were not surprisingly made a great deal harsher by the Fenian outrages in Great Britain itself. To this hardening of opinion in Great Britain two contemporary British beliefs contributed. Much opinion in Britain was firmly in favour of the right to national self-determination, but not very many people believed that this abstract doctrine should be applied to Ireland, however much there might be to be said for it in Poland or Italy. So, for example, *The Times* could in one breath during the Italian crisis of 1859 enunciate the following general principle[9]

> ... The destiny of a nation ought to be determined, not by the opinions of other nations, but by the opinions of the nation itself. To decide whether they are well governed or not ... is for those who live under that government ...

while at the same time continually maintain the need of Ireland for British tutelage. In this happy acceptance of inconsistency most influential British people could readily believe that Fenianism was a further demonstration of unfitness for self-government.

Another contemporary illusion, again very widespread in Great Britain among the governing groups, and again not very realistic, contributed to the abhorrence with which Fenian violence was received. This was the fond but erroneous belief that the British were a law-abiding race on the whole. The society which rejoiced in the suppression of the Indian Mutiny, became alarmed in these years over a series of outrages by trade unionists just about as bad as anything the Fenians perpetrated, and which saw daily in its newspapers a thick layer of vice, cruelty, and violence, nevertheless frequently reflected on its good fortune in having developed a community which was remarkably orderly and law-abiding, with a notable distaste for violence and deep respect for legitimate authority. This illusion contributed to the revulsion which was produced by the killing of Sergeant Brett at Manchester and then

8. *Parliamentary Debates,* CLXXXI, 697.
9. 18-11-1859.

the Clerkenwell explosion. Again the reaction of *The Times* is instructuve; before these events its editorial columns had deplored Fenian activities, but there had still been counsels of moderation, and in particular repeated injunctions not to class all Irishmen with the Fenians, and repeated arguments in favour of leniency on grounds of policy for captured Fenians.[10] "... There cannot be a more fatal mistake than to apply violent remedies to chronic diseases ..."

The Manchester rescue produced immediately a less restrained attitude, partly in the belief that[11]

> ... We have dangerous and violent classes in this country, but the law has attained such a recognized supremacy among us that the officers of the law are seldom seriously obstructed in the discharge of their duty ...

Delane, the editor of *The Times,* immediately hardened his own attitude; he had argued persuasively in favour of commutation of the death sentence on Burke a little while before, but now he sought rather to strengthen the hand of the Government in the case of the "Manchester Martyrs". In private as in the columns of his paper he was firm on this issue. In a letter of 2 November 1867 he wrote :

> ... The Manchester prisoners must be hanged; but they have had the address to make it very difficult and even odious to hang them. Yet the doctrines they avow are absolutely inconsistent with the joint existence of themselves and society, and as society does not mean to be destroyed it is esential that they should be put to death ...

and in obedience to this feeling—which was very far from being confined to Delane—*The Times* duly inserted a weighty editorial in this sense :

10. The change of front by *The Times* is clear from its own columns and also from *John Delane, 1817-1879* by A. I. Dasent, vol. II, pp. 216-8.
  11. 19-9-1867.

... It now remains to consider the question—for it is a question on which public opinion has already been challenged —whether the extreme penalty of the law need be, or ought to be, inflicted upon Allen, Larkin and Gould. We answer, with a deep sense of our duty towards all who may be affected by the ultimate decision, that, in our judgment, it would be an act of criminal weakness to spare the lives of men who have shed innocent blood in the prosecution of an enterprise which aggravates the guilt of murder itself. It has been said that none of them were actuated with a malicious hatred of the courageous man whose life they took because he would not betray his post. The same might be said of almost every murder committed by highwaymen or burglars. Their object is plunder, and not revenge, but they go resolved and prepared to accomplish that object by deadly violence, and they are consigned to the scaffold with the approbation of all communities which maintain capital punishment ...

There can be little doubt that the majority of those who read these words agreed with them, and that the pleas of those who, whether for policy or for humanity, argued for continued leniency were in this crisis ineffective.

Exasperated and angered by the Manchester killing, it is scarcely surprising that opinion in Great Britain reached fever pitch with the Clerkenwell explosion of 13 December, which entirely failed in its main object, but instead inflicted deaths and injuries among men, women and children in the neighbouring working class housing area. Again prevailing sentiment was voiced by *The Times* :[12]

... A crime of unexampled atrocity has been committed in the midst of London ... the slaughter of a number of innocent people; the burning and mangling of women and helpless infants, the destruction of poor men's homes and poor men's property ... It is, indeed, heart-rending to hear of little children four and five years old torn and mangled ... As to the Fenian conspiracy itself, it must be evident that the time is past for clemency and forbearance. With traitors and assassins there can be but one course ...

12. 14 and 16-12-1867.

... The Fenians have cast the glare of a great moral crime upon the debatable ground which separates us, and we can no longer hesitate in which direction to advance. No man deserving of the name will venture to adduce political discontent in palliation of such an outrage ... We are confronted by a gang of reckless criminals, who respect no laws, human or divine ... We must crush them at any cost ...

The Times, which had hitherto been fairly scrupulous in its distinction between Fenians and Irishmen in general, faltered somewhat in these angry days. How could Irishmen perpetrate such atrocities?[13]

... The reason must, we think, be obvious to everybody who has had to do with them, or has even read carefully what any newspaper will tell him. It is the outrageous egotism, the utter selfishness, the shortsightedness, and downright folly of an exaggerated national sentiment ...

In contrast there was, of course, the natural tolerance of the English, partly due to their being a mixed race:
... It is this fusion of races ... that makes the English peculiarly capable of seeing all sides of a political question, of feeling sympathy with all parties, and entering somewhat into the case of those who seem most opposite ... We would live peaceably with all people. We invite all to share our liberty, our opportunities, our comforts, our national greatness ... Of course, we must sometimes suffer the penalty of a generous confidence. Just now we are suffering a little more than usual ...

Not only did the Fenian outrages of 1867 confirm the doubts of those influential elements which had always been more or less hostile to manifestations of Irish nationalist agitation. They went far to alienate a good deal of minority opinion which had been in some degree sympathetically disposed to Irish complaints. *The Spectator* might rebuke *The Times* for confounding all Irishmen

13. 17-12-1867.

grievances which demanded attention,[14] but here too there was with the Fenians, and continue to maintain that Ireland had real nothing but condemnation of Fenianism. Another clear example is provided by Joseph Cowen's *Newcastle Chronicle*,[15] voicing as it did the reaction of radical elements which had for decades sympathised with national aspirations, including those of Ireland.

> ... an outrage as atrocious as it was unprecedented ... the spectacle of infancy and age indiscriminately massacred in obedience to the behests of a patriotism as hollow as it is heartless ... Without the aid of the Liberal element in English society, Ireland cannot possibly achieve her political redemption ... English Liberalism ... cannot grasp a hand which smells rank with the blood of her children, slaughtered in the mere wantonness of fanaticism. Quite as little can it have fellowship with those who smile approval on a spirit so sanguinary. On these points there must be no mistake, and unless Irishmen are prepared to renounce tactics which are rather the tactics of savagery than civilization they must combat alone ...

The British Government never faced serious difficulty in obtaining from Parliament the powers which it needed for the maintenance of its authority in Ireland. The first Act of the Parliament elected in 1865 was the suspension of the Habeas Corpus Act in Ireland; the Bill was introduced on 17 February 1866, passed through both Houses during the day, and received the Royal Assent early the next morning. Fenian outrages made it very easy for renewals of these powers to be obtained from Parliaments determined not to yield to terrorism. The House of Commons gave cold receptions to attempts to move it in favour of Fenian prisoners; in his *Autobiography* Mill records that the reception accorded in the House to his speech in favour of leniency of treatment was such that he and his friends determined that it would be as well if he refrained from speaking at all for some time.[16] Disraeli was surely right in stating that the petition in favour of leniency was[17] "...

14. *Spectator*, 21-12-1867.
15. *Newcastle Daily Chronicle*, 16-12-1867.
16. 1873 edition, p. 288.
17. *Parliamentary Debates*, CLXXXVII, 1904.

disapproved by the entire body of the House, with very rare exceptions ..." *Punch* was guilty of only exaggeration when declaring[18] that the Manchester executions were "made with the approval of all classes worthy of consideration ..." In his *Reminiscences* Justin McCarthy recalled these days as follows :[19]

"... There was a time when the average English mind was suddenly seized with a passion of blended hate, fear and contempt for Fenianism ... It looked more formidable than it afterwards proved to be, and it seemed less like an ordinary rebellious organization than like some demoniacal league against property and public security. When I say seemed, I mean it seemed to the average English mind, to the ordinary society man, and the ordinary shop-keeper ..."

It may not unfairly be concluded that while the Fenian outrages certainly forced British attention for a while to Ireland and her problems they did so at the cost of markedly exacerbating British feeling, and making objective attention to Irish matters more difficult.

It is, moreover, notable how transient the concentration on Fenianism was. In Great Britain, when after the first months of 1868 there was another lull in Fenian activities, little more was heard of them, and even in the crisis months there were many other topics like Reform and Government changes with which Fenianism had to struggle for attention. Certainly among those groups which exercised influence in contemporary Britain the dominant attitude was clearly condemnation of Fenianism, and it is difficult to see how in any way the activities of the Fenians made British public opinion more eager to yield the measures which were necessary to remedy the fundamental grievances of Ireland. The utmost that can be claimed is that Fenianism forced attention on some aspects of Irish feeling for a while. Even the great debate over the Irish Church, however, passed with little reference to Fenianism, and the true indication of the impotence of Fenianism as far as British opinion was concerned must be the fact that the

18. 30-11-1867.
19. Vol. II, p. 211.

legislation of Gladstone's first Government was not very effective in tackling the roots of Irish problems, while even more strikingly indicative was the emptiness of the Irish policy of the Conservative Government of 1874-80. Fenianism had not persuaded or frightened Great Britain into effective action on Ireland's behalf.

It remains to consider some aspects of opinion other than the "mainstream" reaction of "the establishment", for there are one or two areas of British opinion where qualified sympathy for the Fenians can be detected, and even some who were more strongly in favour. It must be stressed, however, that none of these was ever within measurable distance of determining British policy. Inside Parliamentary politics there were one or two men who were deeply concerned and interested in Irish problems, and convinced that Britain still had much to do in this sphere. Cobden died before Fenianism reached its peak, but he had steadily maintained throughout his political career the need for drastic changes in Ireland. Bright remained active, and fearlessly and consistently followed the line that although the worst excesses of Fenianism could not be condoned it must always be remembered that they were not simply the result of natural viciousness but the extreme manifestations of real grievances which should be redressed. In this line of argument he was joined by a brilliant group of intellectuals, including John Stuart Mill, who was the only M.P. who supported Bright on a tense occasion in May 1867 when Bright insisted on reading to a hostile House a petition for lenient and special treatment for Fenian prisoners, submitted by an eminent group which included Frederick Harrison and Professor Beesly—the Professor Beastly of the *Punch* of the day. Justin McCarthy described this petition as follows:[20] "... It really was a very bold thing to do—it was running right in the teeth of the public opinion of all the classes which are called respectable in England," and remarked that because of his part in it Beesly "... was talked of and written of as if he were the advocate and accomplice of assassins ..."

Yet there is no reason to suppose that this little coterie commanded in this attitude any very widespread support; even Mill himself, while normally accorded much respect even from those who

20. *Ibid.*, p. 212.

differed from him, was hardly regarded as a practical man of affairs, but much more as a respected savant. Nor must we suppose that because men like Harrison and Beesly have firm places in the history of British radicalism and played a far from negligible part in helping trade unions, that they attracted wide support among the workers or anywhere else for all their views. There is some truth in a passage from the obituary of Beesly which *The Times* published : [21]

> ... A strong democrat, of a type more common in France than in England, he was always for the masses against the classes. But it may be doubted whether he had much influence over the former ...

Certainly it would be wrong to suppose that Fenianism evoked widespread sympathy among the working classes of Britain. It is true that in the Council of the Reform League there were elements which were willing to side with the Fenians. Odger was the best-known man involved in this line, and also involved in this attempted Fenian—Reform League link was Cluseret, who later played a prominent part in the Paris Commune. So damaging, however, was the idea of such a link to the League's friends in more influential circles that Howell was at great pains to explain away to Thorold Rogers and W. E. Forster some embarrassing sentiments expressed by Odger.[22]

In general there is very little evidence to suggest that there was much sympathy for the Fenians among the British working classes, and on the contrary a great deal more clear evidence of the widespread existence of anti-Irish feeling. Irish immigration into Great Britain produced a difficult problem in integration which, although it was ultimately to be pretty well solved, was certainly still acute in many places in the 1860s. Many of the features of our current problems of integration applied to this earlier situation. In many British towns there were distinct Irish areas—in our contemporary integration problem jargon I suppose they would be called ghettoes—and economic competition, religious

21. 9-7-1915.
22. Royden Harrison, *Before the Socialists,* pp. 83, 141.

differences, and differences in general culture and standard of living all made racial friction endemic in many places. If I may take a handy example from near at hand, although Tyneside was not one of the most noted centres of friction this hostility smouldered throughout the fifties and sixties, on occasion breaking out into violence, sometimes with fatal results. One notable instance, preserved in a local song "The Horrid War i' Sangeyt",[23] involved a most unusual feature. The native inhabitants of one of Newcastle's roughest quarters are only recorded as coming to help the police on this one occasion, and did so in swarms simply because the police were in danger of being overwhelmed by an Irish crowd. There seems ample evidence that during the years of the Fenian troubles anti-Irish feeling was much more common among our working classes than any sentiment of generous sympathy for Irish grievances.

Marx himself provides us with valuable evidence in support of this view.[24] He had high—probably much exaggerated—hopes of the Irish problem as the Achilles' heel of the British ruling classes, but he often expressed his appreciation of the awkward circumstance that the widespread anti-Irish feeling among the workers in Great Britain meant instead an unholy alliance among oppressor and oppressed in Britain to maintain Ireland in subjection.

Marx took a keen interest in the activities of the Fenians and in the late sixties spent a great deal of effort in trying to induce the International to exploit the opportunity Fenianism might be held to present, but it would be absurd to suppose that these activities on his part represented the views of more than a tiny minority in Britain, and in any event his activities in this direction failed to have any very important effect, either on public opinon in Great Britain or anywhere else.

Perhaps the clearest attempt to work up working class demonstrations of sympathy with the Fenians was presented by the meetings held in connection with the trial and execution of the

23. I owe this reference to Mr. C. D. Kilkenny.
24. A number of pertinent letters in *Marx Engels on Britain*, second edition, Moscow 1962, pp. 542 et seq. Also E. H. Carr, *Karl Marx*, pp. 201-2. I am grateful to Dr John Foster for a helpful discussion on this aspect.

Manchester Martyrs.[25] None of these events were very impressive; although Bradlaugh and some of the left-wing elements in the Reform League encouraged these efforts they never amounted to very much, and some of them were dismal failures, such as the attempted meeting at Birmingham on 20 November 1867 which only produced a few hundred people and was punctuated by cries of "Hang 'em".

Nowhere then in British society can any powerful manifestations of sympathy with the Fenians be detected, and indeed it would be surprising in the circumstances if such could be found. The meagre results of their activities in practical effect scarcely justifies Robert Blake's recent remark[26] that they were :

> ... a melancholy example among many others of the efficacy of violence in calling thea ttention of the English to the grievances of their subject peoples ...

The Fenians failed to attract any large or influential body of support at any level of British society, and even if it be admitted that their activities played some part in forcing attention to Irish affairs, the effect was transient, while some of the methods they employed injected further bitterness into Anglo-Irish relationships. It may well be that the old dilemma—disregard in Britain of peaceful Irish representations, and bitter hostility towards Irish illegal activities—meant that the Fenians from the beginning had no chance to achieve anything useful in Great Britain. Certainly after the Machester and Clerkenwell incidents of 1867, there was no chance of a sympathetic hearing in Great Britain to these particular Irish agents; continued trouble in Ireland, and the pathetically abortive attempts on Canada, merely served to confirm British opinion in unrelenting hostility to men whose actions seemed to present a clear challenge to the prevailing conceptions of British society.

25. These efforts are described in a number of newspapers. *The Times* reports them very unfavourably, but there is nowhere any evidence to suggest that they represent any very significant body of opinion. Lord Malmesbury bluntly recorded in his diary that the London meeting of 21-11-1867 was "a failure" (*Memoirs of an ex-Minister*, p. 634). An account of a similar meeting in 1869 is at Dasent, *op. cit.*, p. 250, and is equally unflattering.

26. *Disraeli*, p. 496.

Yet even these strong feelings faded to some degree; although "Fenian" continued as a term of abuse, as new and perhaps more effective Irish champions arose later in the century, the memory of Fenianism faded somewhat in Great Britain, and became rather a part of history than a burning issue. At the turn of the century there was a great flood of popular history books in Great Britain; in their pages the Fenians appeared as wild and impracticable gangsters of the past, and, with Ireland apparently fairly tranquil again, one of them could even claim that[27] ". . . Today our children ask us 'Who were the Fenians?' in the same tone of voice in which they ask ust o enumerate the wives of Henry VIII."

27. E. Hodder, *Life of a Century,* London 1901, p. 548.

FENIANISM AND IRISH POETRY

MALCOLM BROWN

Just before Frank O'Connor died last year, he gave us his opinion on the connection between Fenianism and poetry as follows: "but for an accidental meeting with the old Fenian leader John O'Leary, Yeats might easily have ended as a fine minor poet like Walter de la Mare".[1] O'Connor was not very well Americanized, and by his statement he certainly did not mean what most Americans would; that is, that Yeats required O'Leary's "circus animals" so that he could "desert" them at the proper moment to substantiate his "mature" theme of "disenchantment". The debt O'Connor had in mind was in part the stimulation of the Irish sagas and the Kiltartan dialect, and in part also the stimulation of what Yeats himself described as "the kind of historical crisis which produces literature because it produces passion".[2]

But it takes two to make a transaction, and it was also providential that O'Leary should possess antennae that could sense and evaluate a poetic talent before it had come into existence. At the Dublin Contemporary Club where the two first met in 1885 or 1886, O'Leary offended all the assembled members but one with the pronouncement that the young poet, then twenty or twenty-one, was the only person in the room "who will ever be reckoned a genius". No other Fenian had that percipience, and no other could have given the poet quite the same warmth of welcome.

Fenianism was characterised by a marked doctrinal rigidity tending towards analphabetism. Like every other important historical phase in the Irish struggle for national independence, it took for its starting point the correction of errors that defeated its immediate predecessors. The most ghastly of the recent failures had been Daniel O'Connell's. His "agitation" or verbal frenzy on behalf of the Repeal of the Union in 1843 had terminated in the Famine

1. Frank O'Connor, *A Short History of Irish Literature* (New York, 1967), p. 165.
2. W. B. Yeats, "Modern Ireland", *Massachusetts Review*, vol. no. 2 (Winter, 1964), p. 268.

terror. Fenians took note and drew the lesson that agitational
oratory ought to be banned from all future national movements.
Other Irishmen often tended to agree, and even after eighty years
had passed, James Joyce could still not think of O'Connell's great
gift without bitterness :

> Gone with the wind. Hosts at Mullaghmast and Tara of the
> kings. Miles of ears of porches [i.e., O'Connell=Claudius
> King of Denmark]. The tribune's words howled and scattered
> to the four winds. A people sheltered within his voice. Dead
> noise. Akasic records of all that ever anywhere was. Love and
> laud him : me no more.[3]

The next failures after O'Connell were the Young Irelanders of
1848—Thomas Davis, Gavan Duffy, John Mitchel and Smith
O'Brien. Through their newspaper the weekly *Nation,* they had
floated their message of national rebirth out over the country upon
a wave of song, then went down to ignominious defeat in a comical
effort at insurrection in Tipperary. A study of this misadventure led
Fenians to the more generalised lesson that verbalisations of whatever sort made a "rotten staff" to lean upon. Song was hardly
better than O'Connell's silver tongue. Out of consideration to
tender nerve-ends I will forbear to quote Joyce's highly imaginative
brutality about the lyric patriotism of *The Spirit of the Nation,*
as Young Ireland's song-book was called. Joyce made no distinction between windy O'Connell and windy Davis. But the Fenians
did. Older Fenians had all been Young Irelanders themselves.
Davis's songs and ballads had stirred them once and still ran in
their blood. The "platform spouters" they would never learn to
suffer gladly, but they spared Davis's memory from their sarcasms,
which could be as poisonous as Joyce's own. At the same time,
they found that they could get along without Davis very easily.
In exact opposition to Yeats's famous pontification, "Words alone
are certain good", they evolved a theory of the supremacy of the
deed : deeds alone are certain good. They thought it time for
Irishmen to turn away from "dead voices" to the bare stacatto
phrases that Stephen Dedalus found in Davin's copybook : :

3. James Joyce, *Ulysses* (New York, 1943), p. 141.

—Long pace, fianna! Right incline, fianna! Fianna by numbers, salute, one, two![4]

Each new Irish resurgence in the nineteenth century was a one-man show. Just as Repeal was inseparable from O'Connell "the Liberator", and Home Rule from Parnell "the Chief", so also Fenianism belonged to James Stephens "the Captain". Stephens was a man of astounding capability. He was also a formidable dogmatist, and his organisation provides history with a rare specimen of an extreme left sectarianism that was actually able to stand up and walk. His revolutionary method was to cover the country with a conspiratorial network of secret activists mostly unknown to each other and all subject to his personal command. All other forms of political effort he scorned. He was against petitions, for where had petitions ever got the Chartists? He was against mass demonstrations, O'Connell had used those. He was against parliamentarianism, more O'Connellite humbug. He was against political journalism, for a conspiracy ought not to have a newspaper. But by an accident this last dogma was broken down. In 1863 the Fenian field organisers ran out of cash. Somebody suggested that a newspaper could replenish the cash-box, and so a newspaper was started, called the *Irish People*. Characteristically, Stephens proposed to write all the copy himself, and John O'Leary, the most literate of all the Fenians, was called in merely to watch over the minor mechanical details. In three weeks O'Leary found himself in full command of the paper. Stephens laboured under great pain and produced three leaden leading articles, then fell back exhausted. "He then relapsed into a silence which I never after urged him to break," said O'Leary, for with Stephens's retirement the paper had become his entire responsibility, and remained so for its entire existence of ninety-odd weekly issues.

O'Leary was then thirty-three years old. He had been "out" in the insurrection of 1849 and was jailed but released without being charged. In early manhood he inherited an income that relieved him from the need to work for a living. He went to medical school but took no degree. Mostly he drifted about, indulging his life-

4. James Joyce, *A Portrait of the Artist as a Young Man* (New York, 1928), p. 236.

long passion for book-collecting. About 1860 he met Stephens in an old boarding house in Paris where Irishmen congregated, the same establishment, by an oddity, that has been immortalised in literature under the name of *la maison Vauquer*. The Captain's voluble persuasiveness, which tens of thousands found irresistible, swept him into the Fenian movement.

O'Leary's journalistic model was the old *Nation* of the 1840s under Davis. He hoped to reproduce the paper that had struck him when a lad with the impact that "certain classes of Christians call 'conversion'." (Young John Mitchel's hand used to tremble each week when he tore off the mailing wrapper.) O'Leary admired "O'Donnell Abu", "The Memory of the Dead", "A Nation Once Again", "The West's Asleep", and "The Lament for the Death of Owen Roe O'Neill". Now, nothing is easier than to be arch or witty at the expense of the verse that resulted from Davis's nationalism. A great deal of it actually was exceedingly inept. Even O'Connell, who had no taste at all, complained of the *Nation's* "poor rhymed dullness". Much of the verse was so barren of individuality that the names of the authors could be scrambled without incongruity. Disappointment in the *Nation's* poetry cannot be claimed as an original aesthetic insight. The "de-Davisation" of Irish literature proposed by Yeats in 1894 has not encountered any strong recent opposition. These easy victories over Davis are somewhat beside the point, however. Most of the verses did not survive, and hence are of no concern to anybody. Those that did survive cannot be judged as poems, for the genre to which they belong and in which they earned their success was not poetry, but song in the strict musical sense. Yeats once complained of Tom Moore's melodies that "all but all" were artificial and mechanical "when separated from the music that gave them wings". But except for the limited genre of literary song—"Now Sleeps the Crimson Petal" and the like—any song at all would naturally suffer the same deflation "separated from the music", just as painting may be reduced to banality in black-and-white reproduction. In actuality, many of Davis's songs are indescribably moving and memorable. They "exist". They are not a symptom of the idiocy of the Irish throng nor of its vulgar taste for sub-literature, but stand as a permanent fixture among Ireland's great cultural possessions.

With the soul of an incorrigible bibliophile, O'Leary took up Young Ireland's literary production at the point where it had been interrupted twenty years earlier, hoping to carry on with more of the same. He wasted no time in getting started, and volume one, number one, opened up the literary front with a poem by Robert Dwyer Joyce, the brother of the well-known antiquarian :

> A stricken plain is good to see,
> When victory crowns the patriot's sword,
> And the gory field seemed fair to me
> Won by our arms at Manning Ford.
> 'Twas there we smote them hip and thigh
> 'Till Funcheon's stream ran red with gore,
> 'Till its marge was matted far and nigh
> With the slaughtered bands of Vavasore.[5]

This no-nonsense programme was approved by the public, for the *Irish People* was instantly deluged with a flood of unsolicited patriotic verse. O'Leary believed that his first editorial job, like Gavan Duffy's on the old *Nation*, was to try to turn back the onslaught with biting commentary. In the twelfth issue he wrote :

> We have received this week such a pile of verses that, though very tired we are tempted to give what we were going to call our poetical contributors a few hints. We confess we do this chiefly to save our own time; for though we are usually told that the authors are hard worked, and only write in the intervals of labour, we are afraid they must have too much time to spare, or rather to waste. Ninetenths of the effusions are patriotic. They usually commence by addressing "green Erin", or "dear Erin", or "poor Erin" ... Now, we protest against the right of patriots to write bad verses ... Besides, what is the use of eternally gloating over "slaves" and "chains"! Let them write half the quantity in twice the time. Indeed, we'd rather they only wrote a quarter, but it would be unreasonable to expect that.[6]

5. *Irish People,* 28 November 1863, p. 10.
6. *Irish People,* 13 February 1864, p. 184.

A contributor who signed himself "Young Patriot" was caught trying to palm off one of Davis's poems as his own. O'Leary scolded him and called him a "knave". Another who signed himself "Tyrone" became offensive when his spelling was criticised. He claimed he was being "snubbed" and mistreated. O'Leary replied : "If 'Tyrone' believes what he says of us, why will be persevere in supplying us with prose and verse", and in self-defence he printed one of "Tyrone's" verses :

> Hurrah for the green and the memories green
> Of the red battle-fields of Ireland :
> Hurrah for the brave who there won a grave,
> Defending the cause of our sireland.[7]

He had a feud with one "G.M." who asked to have his verses put first. O'Leary replied, "in the spirit of pure friendship we would advise him to leave off writing verses", and once more he gave a sample to win the reader's sympathy :

> [We] never dreamed the time would quickly come
> When he our youngest, dearest, should "go home".
> My God! how bitter has that parting proved
> To us not him; he did not care to stay.
> His was too fine a nature for the strife—
> The wear and tear—the turmoil of this life,
> Before our eyes he faded day by day;
> Yet still through all, with every feeble breath,
> His love gushed out—'twas only stopped by death.[8]

He had a contretemps with a poetess named "J." "As our fair correspondent requires our impartial opinion upon her verses, we are compelled to say that they are not poetry. They are, however, full of good feeling and most praiseworthy sentiments. We give four lines which, though not poetical, are we hope true" :

> Our Irish maidens now will join,
> With heart and soul and might,

7. *Irish People,* 28 May 1864, p. 424.
8. *Irish People,* 4 June 1864, p. 440.

To forward our lov'd nation's cause,
For which her sons unite.[9]

Meanwhile O'Leary's paper had attracted a number of poetical contributors bearing some measure of reputation. Many had been original members of Davis's own poetical chorus. Many were women : O'Leary's sister Ellen; his cousin "Eva of the *Nation*", who was the wife of Kevin Izod O'Doherty, a patriot who made *Finnegans Wake* thanks to the accident of his middle name; and Parnell's teenage sister Fanny. R. D. Joyce, already quoted, supplied a poem nearly every week, "mostly historical and nearly always warlike". Two of his poets, Thomas C. Irwin and John Francis O'Donnell, are remembered in Geoffrey Taylor's fine modern anthology of nineteenth-century poetry. He also published now and again poems by Charles J. Kickham, already famous for his ballad "Rory of the Hill" and for a song anthologised by Yeats and still sung today after more than a century, the tearful "She Lived Beside the Anner".

Back in the 1840s it had been noted that as soon as any important poet like James Clarence Mangan was assigned to the staff of the old *Nation* or to John Mitchel's *United Irishman,* poetic inventiveness vanished. The *Irish People's* entire professional troupe suffered the same paralysis. Kickham, for example, though far from being feeble-minded, could supply O'Leary's newspaper on demand with nothing better than :

Yes, dearer my sorrowing sireland
Than all the wide world to me;
Oh! I'll cling to my home in old Ireland—
And oh! that dear Ireland were free![10]

In fact, the *Irish People's* professional poets were considerably less interesting than its unsolicited amateurs. Before the paper was a year old O'Leary seems to have discovered that there was more vitality in anonymous ballads and in pure naïveté than he could derive out of talents that were supposedly proved out. Irwin, for

9. *Irish People,* 20 February 1864, p. 200.
10. James Maher, *The Valley Near Slievenamon* (Mullinahone, 1941), p. 164.

example, seems to have sold the *Irish People* the verse he could not
place elsewhere for sufficient reasons, and his "patriotic" verse,
presumably written on command, is quite unreadable. As one looks
back over the old files of the paper, one of the two most striking
specimens of verse is the "Ballad of Billy Byrne", which goes :

> When he was taken prisoner the traitors all came in,
> There was Dixon, Doyle, Toole, Davis, and likewise Bill Dolan,
> They thought it little scruple his precious blood to spill,
> And deprive the county Wicklow of the flower of Pleasant
>   Hill.[11]

Its companion is a one-shot effort by a non-poet, the famous
Fenian O'Donovan Rossa, called "A Soldier's Tale". O'Leary rather
disliked Rossa, and yet he looked back on his poem with something
like wonderment, if not admiration. For myself, I think that if we
did not have Rossa's poem, we would be a trifle poorer (I give
only excerpts) :

> The bailiff with his "notice" came—
> The bit of ground was gone;
> I saw the roof-tree in a flame—
> The crow-bar work was done.

> With neither house, nor bread, nor bed,
> The workhouse was our doom,
> And on my jacket soon I read
> "The Union of Macroom".

> I joined the Red-coats then—*mo léir!*
> What did my father say!
> And I was sent before many a year
> On service in Bombay.

> I thought to be a pauper was
> The greatest human curse;
> But fighting in a robber's cause
> I felt was somewhat worse.

11. *Irish People,* 11 June 1864, p. 456.

I helped to plunder and to slay
Those tribes of India's sons,
And I spent many a sultry day
Blowing Sepoys from our guns.[12]

O'Leary fought against confessing his obvious failure for a long time. In 1886, the year in which he first met Yeats, he was still mulling over the problem in this fashion : "Speranza [Oscar Wilde's mother]' is certainly *not* entitled to the first place among the delightful warblers of her own sex. 'Mary [of the *Nation*]' is entitled to the first place, 'Eva [also of the *Nation*]' to the second."[13] Eventually, though, he surrendered to the reality, and his last statement about the matter was that "the Fenian poets [were] a smaller and weaker band of *literateurs* than the poets of the *Nation*, but one which accomplished something of note in the domain of practical affairs".[14] His discovery made a choice of pains, no doubt, the pain of retreat being probably less than the pain of holding fast to Mary and Eva. Reading back over his weekly budget of poetic gore, he must have felt like any modern reader would feel, or like Joe Gould in Joseph Mitchell's *New Yorker* sketch of long ago, after he had listened to one too many Albanian worker arguingp olitics in a Boston restaurant. "I began to twitch uncontrollably and see double," he said.

O'Leary's real problem was in timing, for he had come too late. The old *Nation* had exhausted the well, a condition that was not readily grasped. Irishmen in later time, especially when hardpressed in retreat, listened for the new magician who, with only a verse or two and a couple of old airs, could turn the tide of their disasters. The demand for ever more piercing exhortation, which was to cause such pain among O'Leary's disciples, became compulsive, as though exhortation was the sovereign cure for all Irish troubles, as though the bugler must be craven who would sound any call but "General Quarters". O'Leary first succumbed to this same temptation, then conquered it. Otherwise, his premise was not absolutely unsound when he argued that "literature must be

12. *Irish People,* 26 December 1863, p. 77.
13. "Historicus", *The Best Hundred Irish Books* (Dublin, 1886), p. 28.
14. In Stopford A. Brooke and T. W. Rolleston, *A Treasury of Irish Poetry* (New York, 1900), p. 199.

national and nationalism must be literary". Chastened and made more flexible his basic proposition went properly to work, as Frank O'Connor reminds us, and in good time it generated world-fabled literary successes. One combination of Fenianism with poetry had made the bad start of

A stricken plain is good to see.

A luckier combination of the same ingredients created that effervescent mixture called the Irish literary movement. Immediately after 1886 it created one of the finest sustained poems of the Romantic movement, which ends :

It were sad to gaze on the blessed and no man I loved of old
    there;
I throw down the chain of small stones ! when life in my body
    has ceased,
I will go to Caoilte, and Conan, and Bran, Sceolan, Lomair,
And dwell in the house of the Fenians, be they in flames or at
    feast.

THE PLACE OF FENIANISM IN THE IRISH REPUBLICAN TRADITION

HEREWARD SENIOR

IF Irish nationalism dates from Strongbow, or even the Danes, Irish republicanism was an offspring of the Volunteers of 1782 and owes much to the external influences of the American and French revolutions. While national feeling undoubtedly existed among the Irish Catholic peasantry at the end of the eighteenth century, it was well in the background and of less concern to them than social and religious questions. Yet these Catholic peasants were the only potential revolutionary force in Ireland, while the Volunteers, amongst whom republicanism arose, were, for the most part, a privileged group who had something to lose from social revolution and much to fear from the religious enthusiasm and long-standing grievances of the Irish majority.

However, the republicans who founded the United Irish Society in 1791, secure in their eighteenth century rationalism, had no fears for they had no doubt but that religion and tradition would soon lise its force witht he people as it had already lost its hold over them. Wolfe Tone wished to abolish "the memory of all past dissensions",[1] not realising that it was more difficult for the injured party to forget the "dead generations" than for the apparent beneficiaries of the conquest. "To fear ihe Catholics," Tone wrote, "is a vulgar and ignorant prejudice," but he added, "look at France and America; the Pope burnt in effigy at Paris, and the English Catholic at this hour seceding from his Church; a thousand arguments crowd at me, but it is unnecessary to dwell on them."[2] As Napoleon's armies marched into Rome, Tone voiced sentiments which would have done credit to an Orangeman ... "I am heartily glad that the old priest is at last laid under contribution; and am strongly tempted to hope that this is but the beginning of his sorrows."[3] On another occasion, Tone wrote, "This country will

1. T. Wolf Tone, *Life and Adventures of,* ed. by his son (Glasgow, n.d.), p. 48.
2. Tone to Chambers, June 1790 (P.R.O.I., Rebellion papers 620/19/24).
3. W. E. H. Lecky, *History of Ireland in the Eighteenth Century* (London, 1892), III, 512.

never be well until the Catholics are educated at home, and their clergy elective".[4] Although Tone expected no serious opposition from the clergy, and consequently contemplated no measures against them, it is clear that he was prepared to countenance a civil constitution of the clergy which, for practising Catholics, could have had the same force as the penal code.

While the Catholic peasantry shared many of the antipathies of the republicans, their view of the world was formed by a vastly different experience, and their methods of struggle were dissimilar. Two of the largest secret societies—the Whiteboys and the Defenders—appear to have included an oath of allegiance to the king in their secret articles. One Whiteboy appeal read, "I declare myself as true and faithful a subject as any in Ireland to both King and Government. In England, when the tenant's lease is expired, no man will dare cast him or his children off their farm, nor will the landlord dream of letting to any other person but the occupier."[5]

But if these secret societies were reluctant to give their agricultural trade unionism the appearance of treason, they had no hesitation in pursuing their ends by a terrorism which was alien to the political habits of republicans. The United Irish state prisoners, Arthur O'Connor, William James MacNeven and Thomas Addis Emmet, wrote of the Catholics that they were considered by the republicans as "entertaining an habitual predilection for monarchy" and "being less attached than the Presbyterians to political liberty".[6] In the same statement, they complained that the Defenders were composed almost entirely of Catholics and those of ... "the lowest order, who, through a false confidence, were risking themselves, and the attainment of redress, by premature and unsystematic insurrection".[7] Assassination, a common secret society practice, was particularly disturbing to the United Irish leaders who considered it "with horror, on account of its criminality ... and if the men at the head of the United Irishmen had thought assassination a justifiable mode of obtaining their ends ... the

---

4. *Ibid.*, III, 354.
5. *Ibid.*, II, 28.
6. W. J. MacNeven, *Pieces of Irish History* (New York, 1807), p. 177.
7. *Ibid.*, p. 179.

poinard would have been directed, not against such petty objects as an obnoxious country magistrate or an informer".[8]

To the republicans, who at first had hoped to provoke a revolution by an openly organised citizens' militia, the attitudes of the Catholic Defenders seemed primitive and their methods self-defeating. Yet these methods, inherited from clan warfare, had been perfected over the generations as a means of redressing particular grievances and punishing individual offenders. It is not surprising, then, that the United Irish programme, which rejected ties of blood and religion, could neither capture the imagination of the Catholic peasantry nor appeal to its self-interest. On their part, the republicans were inclined to look on the Catholic peasants as junior partners in a revolution which would be won mainly by Protestants with French military aid. The growth of the Defender organisation, however, stimulated as it was by faction fights with the Orangemen, created by 1796 what was, in effect, a federation of revolutionary societies which had yet to develop a revolutionary programme. At the same time, government measures had made the growth of legal military clubs impossible and had forced the United Irishmen to organise an underground army.

The failure of the government to take effective action against the Orangemen, in combination with the legal assistance given by republicans on behalf of harrassed Catholics, drove the Defenders into the republican camp and made possible a junction of the two tendencies. Although this resulted in a formidable revolutionary society, commanded by men committed to republican principles, it, in effect, created an organisation in which the spirit of Defenderism prevailed. If there was any chance of keeping the movement under republican control, it was eliminated by General Lake's disarming of Ulster and the arrest of most of the United Irish general staff. What took place in 1798 was a jacquerie in which the republican leaders were virtually prisoners of the forces they led. In the course of creating a powerful revolutionary organisation, the United Irish had, unwittingly, allied themselves with a peasantry moving towards social revolution which, at times, acted as though the uprising was a continuation of the campaign of 1690.

8. *Ibid.*, p. 180.

Although republicanism was to survive in Ulster and among Irish exiles in America, it ceased to be a powerful tendency among Irish Protestants after 1798 and was not to become a force among Irish Catholics again for nearly two generations. If there was any doubt that republicanism was dormant, it was made clear by the collapse of Emmet's *coup d'etat* in 1803. Like his contemporary, Colonel Despard, in London, Emmet anticipated the men of '48 who attempted rebellion without the organisation of an effective network of revolutionary societies. This confidence in spontaneous revolution indicates that, in the minds of the conspirators, at least, a revolutionary tradition had already taken root among the people. While Emmet mistook the restless discontent with the political and social order for active republican sentiment, the republican heroes of '98 and Emmet, himself, were to be remembered with Sarsfield and others who had resisted British rule. A republican tradition thus took its place beside other national traditions, but, for the moment, the peasantry returned to Defender methods of struggle in secret societies, usually described as Ribbonmen who were organised along denominational lines and normally included in their oaths a declaration of loyalty to the crown.[9]

Between the time of Emmet's rising and 1848, republicanism suffered an eclipse on the continent, and was soon to be tarnished in America by the issue of slavery, while a religious revival was to give new strength to the Church. Although Daniel O'Connell had little in common with the United Irish, like them, he was able for a time to divert the energies of most of the peasantry from limited secret society methods towards a national political activity and enabled them to create in the "Liberators" a para-military organisation similar to the Volunteers. O'Connell's Catholic Association and subsequent repeal movement stood in the same relation to the men of '48 as the United Irish did to the Volunteers. Yet O'Connell's victory in 1829 marked a return of the peasantry to Ribbonism which they had never wholly abandoned. As the young men who conspired in 1848 were more familiar with general ideas, often borrowed from the continent, than with the outlook of the peasantry, they were inclined to blame O'Connell's want of

9. Evidence of Daniel O'Connell, *Report on the State of Ireland, Report from the Select Committee with Minutes of Evidence*, H.L. 1825 [181], IX, 147-8.

aggressiveness for what was perhaps an absence of strong national sentiment among the people. They therefore sought to remedy O'Connell's supposed weaknesses by taking a stance of defiance.

Smith O'Brien was a hesitant republican converted somewhat reluctantly by the renaissance of republicanism in continental Europe. His idea of revolution was a rising of the peasantry under patriotic landlords.[10] James Fintan Lalor was really the only doctrinaire republican of '48 and the only leader anxious to harness the forces of social revolution to the fortunes of an Irish republic. He urged that rents be withheld from landlords who refused to support the national cause, and was prepared to see their property confiscated as had been that of the American loyalists after the revolution.[11] While this programme undoubtedly had possibilities, it would require patient work among the peasantry, which was not in the spirit of '48, and, above all, it required links with Ribbonism and a partial adoption of its methods, which was incompatible with the chivalrous ideals of the "Young Irelanders". While the men of '48 became conspirators, theirs was essentially an open conspiracy which would prepare Irishmen for rebellion by a diffusion of military knowledge, by encouraging them to acquire arms, and by organising a series of political clubs. Such methods left the initiative to the government which could and did arrest the leaders at will.[12]

Perhaps the most misleading circumstance of '48 was the manner in which the people were prepared to defend the republicans against arrest and the way in which crowds responded to nationalist oratory—sympathy with the enemies of established authority could and was easily mistaken for a willingness to make sacrifices for independence. For the few who turned out for active service, there were prospects of neither loot nor pay, nor help from abroad, and if the barricade revolutions based on capital cities were to fail on the continent, barricades in provincial towns were ludicrous. The republicans of '48 were not formidable, nor were they taken very seriously by the authorities. There was less of the

10. Charles Gavan Duffy, *Four Years of Irish History* (Paris, 1883), pp. 645-6.

11. *Ibid.*, pp. 464-532, 761; see also Denis Gwynn, *Young Ireland and 1848* (Cork, 1949), pp. 128-38.

12. Duffy, *Four Years of Irish History*, pp. 606-700; Gwynn, *Young Ireland and 1848*, pp. 239-67.

tragedy of '98 but enough to lend substance to the republican tradition—republicans had confronted troops on barricades and there was exile and imprisonment for the leaders. Moreover, a new dimension had been added to Irish politics by the growth of the emigrant population in America. Ribbonism had taken roots there in the twenties when Ribbonmen clashed with Orangemen in New York.[13] Ribbonism and other secret societies were eminently suited to the needs of Irishmen in the new world as a means of keeping Irishmen together and of exploiting the advantages of combination. In the United States there would be a growing body of Irishmen who became republican when they became American and would, with the encouragement of Anglophobe politicians, provide moral and material support to Irish republicans. Henceforth, there were to be resources available to maintain a republican movement which was not a mere reflection of revolutionary tendencies fashionable in continental Europe, but which had a permanent base and permanent organisation. Once established, it would experiment with modes of struggle popular at the time, and in the age of Garibaldi, John Brown and William Walker, Irish revolutionaries would find filibustering expeditions attractive.

Although the obvious leaders of a new Irish republican movement were the Young Irelanders of '48, like the United Irish leaders, they were men of considerable education and ability who would not find revolutionary conspiracy an attractive occupation in an age when it had no immediate prospect of success. Talented literary men had failed as conspirators in '48, and conspiracy seemed to be the only recourse of avowed republicans determined upon an armed uprising. Less conspicuous men were needed, men willing to accept the authority of those less able than themselves. A professional revolutionary organisation seemed most likely to be effective, and it was this type of organisation which James Stephens and his followers attempted to create in 1858 later called the Irish Republican Brotherhood.[14]

If an effective underground military organisation was to be established among social elements normally attached to Ribbonism,

13. *Colonial Advocate*, Queenston, Upper Canada, 18 Nov. 1824.
14. The American counterpart assumed the name of Fenian Brotherhood in 1859, a name later applied to the entire movement.

attention would have to be given to economic questions. While Stephens had a social programme calling for land reform and even nationalisation of Church property, emphasis on social questions had its dangers. It would be folly to neglect legal methods of struggle or co-operation with non-republicans in efforts to improve the immediate condition of the people. Yet the difficulty of combining legal methods and moderate allies with preparations for an armed uprising was manifest. And the use of Ribbon methods for redressing local grievances by terrorism could no more be encouraged by the Fenians than by the United Irish, as secrecy was essential and sporadic violence endangered the grand strategy of the conspirators. Moreover, a policy of redressing economic grievances, either by legal methods or terrorism, would have little romantic appeal to Irish Americans who expected nothing less than the humiliation of England by military defeat.

America was to play the role in Fenian plans which France had in those of the United Irishmen. While Wolfe Tone had hoped to co-ordinate a primarily Protestant rising with a French invasion, the Fenians looked forward, in the words of one of their poets, to the time "when Yankee guns shall thunder on Britain's coast and land our green flag under the Fenian host".[15] Although the Fenians had a series of projects rather than a master plan, it was generally expected that Irish Americans would offer financial assistance and trained officers to organise the Irish underground, and perhaps despatch a filibustering expedition, while doing what they could by propaganda and other pressures to damage Anglo-American relations. Negotiations with all potential enemies of Britain were sought as a matter of course, with Stephens looking to Napoleonic France and considering the possibility of a life president for Ireland,[16] which raised doubts about the depth of his republicanism. Yet it was only in the United States that the Irish vote could offer a means of exerting effective influence in a powerful state.

A revolutionary conspiracy such as the Fenians planned could hardly work in harmony with the Church which had denounced

15. John Rutherford, *The Secret History of the Fenian Conspiracy* (London, 1877), p. 162.
16. *Ibid.*, p. 290.

all secret societies since the days of the Whiteboys. The Fenians suffered rather more from such denunciations than did societies organised along denominational lines, especially as they had men of Protestant background like John Mitchel, Thomas Clarke Luby and James Stephens, himself, among their leaders and many Catholics who maintained close associations with anti-clerical republicans on the continent. Discord between the movement and the Church imposed serious but unavoidable limitations on the Fenians who had only to recall the events of '48 to realise the dangers of working in the face of clerical disapproval. Yet, as Archbishop Hughes of New York pointed out at the funeral service for MacManus in 1861, the Church would countenance rebellion only when it was just, popular, and had a chance of success.[17] As there was little prospect of the last condition being realised, those engaged in armed conspiracy had to be and were, in fact, reconciled to tension with the Church hierarchy, which would be more acute in Ireland than in republican America.

Yet, however much the Fenians might resent the attitude of the clergy, they were nott o echo the sentiments of Wolfe Tone in the previous century. The Church was now recognised as a formidable power which was not expected to wither away in the near future. Although continental republicans were hostile to the Church, this mattered little to the Fenians who were more concerned with republican conspiracy than republican doctrine. The republicanism of Wolfe Tone, who did not hesitate to condemn Americans for want of republican virtues, was more profound, and while among the men of '48, Fintan Lalor might have become a Mazzini, the Fenian leaders were cast more in the mould of Garibaldi. As the Fenians were primarily men of action, their contribution to the republican tradition would be in deeds which would draw the attention of their contemporaries and future generations to the idea of an Irish republic. With their picnics, conventions and para-military organisations, they provided for the social needs of the less assimilated Irish Americans, while in Irish politics they became an intrusive element which would create difficulties for moderate nationalists and harden the attitude of Ulster towards home rule.

17. *Ibi*d., pp. 189-90.

In the relative calm of the fifties and sixties, it was impossible for Stephens to organise an underground army of the proportions of the United Irish army. In the face of a police force, less terrifying but more efficient than the disorganised crown forces of '98, there was little chance of reanimating latent fears of an Orange massacre. Informers remained a serious problem and measures taken against them undermined the mutual confidence of the republicans. The financial scandals and the comic aspects of Fenianism, often deliberately over-played by the conspirators to quiet the fears of the authorities, alienated the educated classes. While the men of '48 had entertained illusions about a spontaneous mutiny of the Irish in the British army,[18] the Fenians had made patient efforts to encourage desertions and to plant cells in British regiments,[19] as the Defenders and United Irish had in '98. Such efforts, certainly more deserving than the shallow optimism of '48, were futile, though the hope the Fenians sustained of securing the neutrality of assistance of the military was undoubtedly good for Fenian morale.

In spite of the elaborate planning and support of the Fenian organisation in America, ther ebels of '67 were no more successful than the men of '48. There was no jacquerie as in '98 because the Fenians had not succeeded in harnessing the latent power of Ribbonism, even though they often incorporated Ribbonmen into their organisation. With the failure in Ireland in '67 and the collapse of the filibusters against Canada in 1866 and 1870, the prospect of establishing an Irish republic through a Fenian agency was clearly gone. Fenianism and the institutions which emerged from it survived because conspiracy and propaganda had become a way of life for men who had given up the hope of interesting careers along more conventional lines. With the coming of Parnell and the Land League, the energies of the peasant, which the Fenians had failed to exploit, were turned towards economic ends —something more comprehensible to the peasantry than the idea of an Irish republic. And, as land reform gradually eliminated the possibility of using agrarian discontent, Fenian conspiracies became more imaginative and less effectual. Of these, perhaps the

18. Duffy, *Four Years of Irish History*, p. 648.
19. Rutherford, *Fenian Conspiracy*, pp. 103-5.

building of a Fenian submarine,[20] anticipating the U-boat, was the most romantic.

By the late sixties, Fenianism, which had never had a single recognised head, disintegrated into a series of factions with little control over the ordinary members. The killing of D'Arcy McGee[21] was an early example of the re-emergence of the kind of assassination committee which the United Irish republican leaders had specifically disavowed. More spectacular were the Phoenix Park murders by the Invincibles, which represented not only a departure from republican policy but from Ribbon practice in that the victims were killed simply as representatives of the established order. And it is significant that although there was virtually no sympathy for the Invincibles, there was a good deal for the assassin who killed the informer responsible for their arrest. Fenian activities at this time were compared by a contemporary French writer[22] to those of the Russian Nihilists and parallels undoubtedly existed. Yet Fenianism was essentially a popular movement in which general ideas counted little and systematic terrorism was seldom employed.

In the age of Home Rule, violence was going out of fashion, but it returned in 1914,r e-animating what appeared to be a dying republican tendency. Indeed, volunteering itself was to be revived by Carson and with it, the idea of barricade revolution by citizen militia. The Easter Rising was in the tradition of Robert Emmet, of '48 and '67, perhaps more of '48 than '67 in spite of the American connection, as the men of 1916 were hardly professional revolutionaries. Yet this gesture of the lineal descendants of the Fenians was to unleash a new kind of warfare in which professional revolutionaries were at last to act in the spirit of Ribbonism. Terrorism was finally employed on a national scale with clearly defined revolutionary objectives. Assassination would silence informers and police were attacked as symbols of the state. While the acceptance of the Treaty by Michael Collins and the sub-

20. John Devoy, *Devoy's Post Bag*, ed. William O'Brien and Desmond Ryan (Dublin, 1948), I, 470-2.

21. H. Senior, "Quebec and the Fenians", in *Canadian Historical Review*, vol. XLVIII, no. 1, March 1967, pp. 39-44.

22. A. Leroy-Beaulieu, "Les Sociétés Secrètes en Irlande", in *Revue politique et littéraire*, vol. I, Jan.-July 1881, pp. 545 ff.

sequent failure of the rebels in the civil war suggest that such tactics have their limitations, they were by far the most effective used in the history of Irish republicanism. Yet, although the success of these tactics owed much to republican-inspired propaganda, the tactics themselves owed more to the spirit of the Whiteboys, Defenders and Ribbonmen than to the men of '98, '48, the Fenians, or even the men of 1916. It is significant, perhaps, that Michael Collins and General Mulcahy were not doctrinaire republicans and, like the Ribbonmen, were prepared to take an oath of allegiance to the crown. Moreover, there were few who fought in 1916 or in the War of Independence who were not practising Catholics, indicating the degree to which Irish republicans had moved away from the rationalist United Irishmen and even from the early Fenian leaders.

The United Irishmen gave republicanism a place in the Irish national tradition which was confirmed by the Young Ireland movement of '48. But, had it not been for the Irish Americans, it is doubtful that this tradition would have given rise to a permanent republican organisation at a time when revolutionary idealists were turning towards social and national questions. Although the existence of a large Irish population in the United States made a republican movement of some kind almost inevitable, it was the Fenian leaders who determined its non-intellectual, conspiratorial and quasi-military character. Undoubtedly, this approach offered the best prospect of harnessing the forces of agrarian revolt to the republican cause, was acceptable to many Irish Americans, and was most congenial to those who had served in the American Civil War. Yet, if Fenianism kept republicanism alive, it tended to rally the enemies of Irish nationalism, it alienated men of high intelligence like D'Arcy McGee and it embarrassed moderates. Finally, the institutions which grew out of Fenianism—the Irish Republican Army and the Clan na Gael—ensured that there would be a token force of republicans to take the field when revolution again became fashionable.

D'ARCY McGEE AND THE FENIANS

A STUDY OF THE INTERACTION BETWEEN IRISH NATIONALISM AND THE AMERICAN ENVIRONMENT

ROBIN B. BURNS

THE incidents connected with the Fenian raids have acquired a certain status in the Canadian national heritage. The popular view sees Canadians of diverse creeds and backgrounds coming together to assert their new Confederation against the invaders from the south. Like 1812, it has become another example when Canadians defended their right to a separate and distinct existence on the North American continent. Historians have accepted the invasions as indispensable to the accomplishment of Confederation in 1867. The pro-Confederation forces made the Fenians out to be a real and present danger to the survival of British North America. When faced with possible annexation, Confederation became the lesser of two evils to those who were reluctant to accept the new union. In fact, one terrorist incident coincided so exactly with the New Brunswick election on the issue of Confederation, that some contemporaries suspected a conspiracy between the pro-Confederation forces and the Fenian leaders. And one historian, C. P. Stacey, who laments the sectionalism of Canada today, recently thought it a pity that the Fenians chose to disband, for it removed one of the external forces keeping Canadians together.

By his determined opposition to Fenianism, D'Arcy McGee won a special position as a Canadian hero. His assassination in 1868, at the hands of a Fenian, became the crowning glory of a career that Canadian nationalists make to personify the Canadian experience. To a romantic Canadian nationalist, McGee's career can be interpreted as follows. With Young Ireland, McGee dabbled in the heresies of European nationalism and liberalism. Exiled to the United States, he soon became disillusioned with that other heresy, republican democracy. His journey to Canada represented the end of this wandering in the desert, for he recognised the integrity of Canadian institutions and the superiority of its social order. An early advocate of Confederation, he became the "prophet of Canadian nationality". His stand against Fenianism, with its American and republican overtones, demonstrated the depths of that nationalism and subordination of his Irish heritage to it. With his assassination, he became "Canada's first political martyr" and inspired the "apostles of Canada First" who continued the struggle for Canadian survival.

D'Arcy McGee and Fenianism has another significance. In his history of Fenianism in the United States, William D'Arcy described McGee's opposition to the movement as the main factor in the failure of the Canadian Irish to join in the liberation of their native land. Since the assumption that the Canadian Irish would rise was vital to the success of the invasion, the history of Fenianism must account for McGee's opposition, and for Irish Canada's reluctance. Moreover, McGee had been active in both the United States and Ireland before coming to Canada. He had helped to edit the *Nation,* he had been secretary for the Irish Confederation, he had been responsible for organising the clubs in the Irish League, and he had been arrested in 1848. Before 1848, he had worked for the Boston *Pilot.* Later, he edited the New York *Nation,* and *American Celt* in Boston and Buffalo. As McGee's opposition to Fenianism emanated to a large extent from that experience, this minor episode in the national history of a British dependency is an integral part of Irish and American history. McGee is a key figure to test the nature of the interaction between the American environment and Irish nationalism.

There have been several ways of accounting for McGee's apparent endorsement of Irish revolution in 1848 and his decision to battle it twenty years later. Irish and American nationalists saw him as one who had sold hisr evolutionary soul for the sake of personal gain. They emphasised his continuous inability to manage his financial affairs. They explained his declining radical and anti-clerical opinions after 1848 by alluding to the influence of clerical money helping to revive a dying newspaper. When McGee began to attack republicanism and defend the British connection in Canada, the New York *Tribune* echoed this theme :

> The democratic tarantella which Mr. McGee used to dance so beautifully has been entirely cured by the jingling of Treasury silver ... about this time, Thomas will be getting ready to be made Sir Thomas ... and so we leave him, with

the galling consolation, that in any posture of affairs, he can always make a speech, upon either side of any question.[1] Canadian nationalists preferred to see him as a young man distraught by the Great Famine and carried away with the euphoria of that revolutionary era. The condition of the Irish in the eastern cities of the United States and the realities of American politics opened his eyes to the errors of republicanism and prepared him to embrace the Catholic Church and Canadian nationalism as conservative alternatives.

A third, and more recent, interpretation denied that McGee was ever a revolutionary. D. C. Lyne pointed to McGee's basic conservative position in the Young Ireland movement. He emphasised McGee's support within the Irish Confederation for Smith O'Brien and Gavan Duffy against John Mitchel, Devin Reilly and Fintan Lalor. Lyne viewed McGee's opposition to Fenianism as the extension of that factional division to 1867 and North America. Lyne also stressed the importance of local politics in explaining why McGee chose to be so vehement about Fenianism. By identifying local opposition with the Fenian threat, Lyne claimed that McGee succeeded in discrediting and defeating a local threat to his leadership of Irish Canadians. Or as one of McGee's local contemporaries put it in a threatening letter :

> You turncoat . . . when you were editor of the *New Era* you were as big a rebel as ever uttered a lie . . . and now you turn around and call the Fenians a lot of rascals and dupes, because they are trying to free themselves from the yoke of England . . . The whole object you have in view is to become popular . . .[2]

As the last argument tends to undermine the validity of this paper, I will have to consider it first. When McGee arrived in Philadelphia following the failure in 1848, he wrote a lengthy public letter. Basically it was a reply to those critics who had charged that Young Ireland had been hasty and irresponsible in

1. *New York Tribune,* quoted in the *Christian Guardian,* 2 September 1863.
2. Public Archives of Canada, D'Arcy McGee Papers, J. J. Sullivan to T. D. McGee, 23 November 1865.

calling for armed resistance to British policy. McGee argued that the Irish League did have a significant organisation and a rational plan of operations. As the co-chairman of the committee responsible for organising rifle clubs, he claimed the existence of five hundred clubs with a total membership of thirty thousand.

> Each club, [he continued], was divided into sections of ten men, with a master to each section, who knew, personally, each of his ten men ... these sections nearly all exist, and form a nucleus of future movement which cannot be reached or crushed.[3]

McGee noted that their strength was confined to the urban areas. During the resistance, however, the fight had to be carried to the rural areas where, imitating the tactics of the Spaniards against Napoleon, the concentrations of British troops would be vulnerable. The rural population had failed to support the League, because the clergy had failed to co-operate with its leaders. Nevertheless, with the rifle clubs still intact, and stands of arms uncaptured, the Irish were ready to win "Freedom's battle" in the near future.

> That it will be won in Ireland, [he concluded], and sooner than many, even among her friends, dare hope, I believe. The vice of loyalty is gone at the root, and it but needs a little more of time's teaching to make a democratic revolution, which will wait for no leadership to strike to make Ireland as free as the freest ... Thomas D'Arcy McGee (A traitor to the British Government).[4]

McGee continued his appeal for Irish revolution, and his attacks on the Catholic clergy in the editorials of his New York *Nation*. He campaigned for American intervention on behalf of European nationalities. He also turned his attention to Canada. He called on the Irish there to join with the French Canadians and establish a democratic republic.

3. *Boston Pilot,* 21 October 1848.
4. *Ibid.*

Brethren! we look to you to protect yourselves, and avenge
the famines of '46, '47, and '48, on their heartless authors ...
Never had men a holier cause. England has ruled you for a
century, and at the end of it you find yourselves ruined? Are
you content? Are you happy? Are you not slaves? Never had
men a holier cause. You strike at the empire in the name of
all its victims. Let the green flag be your banner, and your
war-cry, "remember Ireland".[5]

From the evidence just cited, it seems legitimate to conclude that
in 1848 and 1849 McGee had gone beyond the limited nationalism
of Davis, Duffy and Smith O'Brien, to endorse an Irish republican
revolution. Moreover, he specifically proposed tactics which were
later adopted by the Fenians in Ireland and the United States.

The first critical aspect of McGee's change to an anti-revolu-
tionary position was evident when he altered his attitude towards
the Catholic Church. By 1850 his editorials had initiated a public
controversy with Archbishop Hughes of New York and had terminated in the condemnation and failure of his newspaper. Decid-
ing against returning to Ireland, he began a new journal in
Boston, the *American Celt*. In 1852 when Thomas Francis
Meagher escaped to the United States, McGee published an open
letter where he criticised his former nationalist position. In a series
of statements which bordered on a public confession, he maintained
that the Irish had been misled by English and French principles.

Since Burke died, politics ceased to be a science in our island
and in England. The cruel political economy of Adam Smith
never had disciples among us; the eloquence of Sheil is not
bottomed upon any principle; the *ipse dixit* of O'Connell
could be no substitute to ardent and awakened intellects for
the satisfying fullness of a Balmes or a Brownson.[6]

In arguing for a return to first principles within an Irish
tradition, he concluded by a profession of faith in the Catholic
Church and a determination to resist, "... the conspirators who,

5. *Nation* (New York), 31 March 1849.
6. *American Celt,* August 1852, quoted in I. Skelton, *The Life of
Thomas D'Arcy McGee* (Garden City 1925), p. 195.

under the stolen name of Liberty, make war upon all Christian institutions".[7] McGee's pro-Catholic and conciliatory attitude in his new journal provoked the charge that he had sold out to the Archbishop of Boston to meet the loss he had sustained with the *Nation*.

If one is to arrive at an accurate evaluation of McGee's position, however, one has to put his new profession of faith within its American context. His letter to Meagher coincided with a growing interest in the Irish American immigrant. From 1842 to 1845 when he worked for the Boston *Pilot*, McGee had been concerned about the position of the Irish in American society. Like many, he saw the American experiment as the chance for the Irish to demonstrate that, given equal rights and opportunity, they would become leading and responsible citizens. He had participated in the campaign against nativism. At the age of twenty he had written a book entitled *O'Connella nd his Friends* to give the immigrants a sense of history and identity.

From the beginning of his second residence in the United States, however, he had become interested in more immediate social problems. To McGee the conditions of the Irish in New York and Boston seemed to be characterised by ignorance, poverty, intemperance, corruption and slums. Nativists blamed the Irish Catholic character. Irish Americans pointed to intolerance and discrimination. To McGee the Irish had exchanged one kind of misery in Ireland for another in the United States. In his *History of the Irish Settlers in North America,* published in 1850, he described the hazards of immigrant life and concluded, "An East Indian suddenly left on a cape of Labrador would not pass more visibly from one condition of being to another than the Irish emigrant who finds himself new landed in America".[8]

Shortly after his arrival in New York, McGee began to concentrate less on replying to nativist charges and more on trying to remedy social problems affecting the Irish immigrant. He helped organise rifle clubs in New York to encourage self-reliance and self-help. He worked to establish adult education centres. By 1856, after

7. *Ibid.,* p. 195.
8. T. D. McGee, *A History of the Irish Settlers in North America,* sixth edition (Boston 1855), p. 235.

lecture tours in Canada West and the American interior, he began
to hold the American cities responsible for the destruction of the
family fabric and the corruption of Irish values. In the editorials
of the *American Celt* he campaigned for extensive immigration to
the west. He dreamed of a St. Patrick's in the Woods, somewhere
in Illinois, where the Irish would return to the land under the
pastoral care of their clergy, and recover their lost identity. He
called for an Irish immigrant land company to sell shares to
prosperous Irishmen, and buy land in the west. It would provide
easy terms of credit for Irish immigrants, and encourage western
settlement. He surveyed sources of capital and available land.
As chairman of the Finance Committee of the Irish Immigrant
Aid Convention held in Buffalo in 1856, McGee had his report
and programme accepted.

McGee's reaction to American society coincided with his new
attitude towards Catholicism. In his book *The Catholic History of
North America* he defined a new role for the Irish immigrants, this
time in American terms. In a developing society, he saw the Irish
and their Church as an instrument for the conservation of traditional values on the North American continent. At the same time
he openly criticised the Irish American nationalists. He described
them as irresponsible demagogues who were exploiting the immigrant and drawing his attention away from real issues. In one
public lecture he demanded, "Why don't they liberate the Ireland
at their own doors, from the poisonous and murderous surround-
ings of the tenement houses of New York and Boston?"[9] Drawing
from the American experience, he now attacked the republican
revolutionary solution for Ireland as breaking with her fundamental historical identity. To McGee, republicanism had destroyed Irish values in the United States. Might it not have the
same effect in Ireland?

> The true "Irish Cause" is not now and never was, a revolu-
> tionary cause. It is purely historical in its origins, and con-
> servative in its objects; ... it aims at *restoration* not at *revolu-
> tion* ... The politics of Irish patriots, in our humble judg-

9. Public Archives of Canada, John O'Gorman Papers, "McGee the
Irishman, Canadian, and Catholic", p. 5.

ment, would [be] ... to substitute a free, federal union, for the present tyrannical, imperial incorporation.[10]

While it is legitimate to trace the origins of McGee's anti-Fenian position to a romantic view of Irish history and to his disillusionment with revolutionary principles as they applied to the Irish in the United States, one can exaggerate these as explanatory factors accounting for McGee's decision to move to Canada. By 1855 McGee had come to appreciate the differences between British rule in Ireland and British rule in Canada. However, his move to Montreal was comparable to his change from New York, to Boston, to Buffalo, and back to New York between 1848 and 1857. Financially, they were attempts to recover from a desperate situation. Ideologically, they were attempts to find acceptance for his views and to influence opinion. Although his Montreal newspaper was optimistically entitled the *New Era,* his editorials contrasted little with those of his American journals. He campaigned for greater Irish representation in Canadian affairs, while condemning the influence of the Orange Order as a kind of British North American nativism.

Six years later, McGee was beginning to emphasise the differences between the Canadian and American historical experiences. While the United States was bitterly divided and engaged in a bloody Civil War, McGee began to outline the historical basis for a Canadian nationality. In 1849 the local representative of the British Crown had signed into law a measure passed by the Canadian Assembly. The Rebellion Losses Bill provided public money to compensate those who had suffered property damage at the hands of British troops in the rebellion of 1837. With the Canadian government now responsible to the Canadian Assembly, Canada had achieved self-government without a revolution and without a republican declaration if independence. In the years that followed, the landholding system was reformed, the seigneurial system was abolished, and the Anglican Church was disestablished. French was made an official language. A public school system was inaugurated, yet separate religious schools were provided for by the state. To McGee, the Canadians had achieved everything that

10. *American Celt,* quoted in the *True Witness,* 19 May 1854.

the Americans had, without a break from the British Empire, without a radical separatgon of Church and State, and without the ascendancy of one racial or religious group. For McGee's own situation, perhaps the greatest manifestation of what this new political society meant, was when the former traitor to the British government was sworn in as a Canadian minister of the British Crown.

By 1863 McGee was becoming one of the leading spokesmen for the consolidation of the Canadian experience into a confederation and a new nationality. He had used Burke's definition of a nation for the motto of his New York *Nation,* "A nation is a moral essence, not merely a geographic expression or a distinction of nomenclature".[11] He now applied that definition to the Canadian situation. Along with their neighbours to the south, Canadians shared the liberty and freedom which McGee described as indigenus ploants of North American soil. However, with constitutional monarchy and parliamentary government, Canadians had worked out a more effective balance between this natural freedom and the principles of law and authority. In a manifesto of his political philosophy, McGee declared, "I take it for granted that everyone ... will admit two things to be essential to good government—stability and freedom".[12] He went on to account for the American difficulties in those terms.

> ... in open revolt against what they considered—and in my opinion rightly considered—the excesses and oppressions of ancient authority—[the Founding Fathers] were so busy looking after their new found liberty, they forgot, they too, could not long govern without authority.[13]

He described the American Civil War, riots in the cities, American nativism, and the corruption of political parties, as symptoms of this general shortcoming. In two articles entitled "A Plea for British American Nationality", he elaborated on this theme and insisted, "We are arrived at that stage of experience, and we find ourselves surrounded by experiences which enable us to play an

11. *Nation* (New York), 31 March 1849.
12. *Gazette* (Montreal), 3 July 1863.
13. *Ibid.*

essentially different part from that forced on the revolted colonies of 1776".[14] McGee became the first Canadian to carry that plea to the Atlantic Provinces, urging the incorporation of these principles into a Confederation of British North America.

> ... I invoke the fortunate genius of a united British America, to solemnize law with the moral sanctions of religion, and to crown our fair pillar of freedom with its only appropriate capital, lawful authority, so that, hand in hand, we and our descendents may advance steadily to the accomplishment of a common destiny.[15]

Just as he had enunciated a role for the Irish in American society, McGee began to speak of a role for the Irish in the Canadian national experience. Under the British flag in North America they supported their own Church, enjoyed a public education in state supported separate schools, had representatives at all levels of government, and experienced relatively peaceful co-existence with other religious and national groups. Within this environment, McGee called on the Irish to render a double service.

> We, Irishmen, Protestant and Catholic, born and bred in a land of religious controversy, should never forget that we now live and act in a land of the fullest religious and civil liberty.[16] For us, the Irish in Canada, there is at least this one public duty, clear beyond doubt, namely to show, both for the sake of our adopted and our native country, that it is possible, aye, that it is most natural, that we should dwell together in peace as one people.[17]

14. T. D. McGee, "A Further Plea for British American Nationality", *British American Magazine,* vol. I (1863), p. 564.

15. T. D. McGee, "The Common Interests of British North America", 31 July 1863, in T. D. McGee, *Speeches and Addresses Principally on the Subject of British American Union* [hereafter, *Speeches and Addresses* ...], (London 1865), p. 67.

16. T. D. McGee, "American Relations and Canadian Duties", 10 May 1862, *Speeches and Addresses* ..., p. 36.

17. T. D. RcGee, "Irish National Standing or Reputation", *Speeches and Addresses* ..., p. 143.

Moreover, while the American Civil War was contributing to the deterioration of Anglo-American relations and creating a threat to Canadian survival, he called on the Irish to join an Irish Regiment in the Canadian militia.

> ... the Irish have no grievance in Canada. Have you any state Church here, or landed aristocracy to turn out the peasant upon the highway by summary ejectment? Then if you have no complaint, is it not your duty, as it is that of all other nationalities, to stand by the government and give the highest practical proof possible that an Irishman well governed becomes one of the best subjects of the law and of the sovereign?[18]

Into this situation came the Fenians with their cry for the Canadian Irish to join in the liberation of their native and adopted countries from the tyranny of British rule. From as early as 1860, when McGee became aware that Fenianism was making its presence felt in Canadian circles, he began to combat it both secretly and publicly. He recommended that the Canadian Prime Minister appoint an agent in the United States who would infiltrate the Fenian organisation and provide intelligence. In the Cabinet he urged the reform of the Canadian militia, and their reinforcement by British troops. As 17 March 1866 approached, he worked to have St. Patrick's Day demonstrations suspended in Canada.

As an Irish Canadian spokesman he also used his influence to have local groups resist the Fenian threat. In public letters and in public addresses he suggested that Irish communities establish committees to expose local Fenians and have them removed from positions of influence. He recruited for the Irish Regiment and was made president of the Loyal Irish Canadian Society. He argued that if the Irish responded favourably to the Fenian appeal it would turn Protestnat against Catholic. It would also jeopardise the future of the Irish in Canadian society.

18. T. D. McGee, "Canada Considered as a Whole", *Gazette* (Montreal), 9 December 1865.

If this root of suspicion of treason should strike into our ranks, then no good subject of this country—no lover of Canada or her laws could encourage the settlement of another Irishman among us. No public office which could be filled by anyone else—no professional patronage, no social recognition, no office of trust, no magisterial duty, could be or would be entrusted to one of the suspected denomination.[19]

Following the raids in 1866, McGee called for the full prosecution of the Fenian captives. When a Catholic priest from Kingston wrote to McGee and asked him to intervene on behalf of a local resident who had been implicated on one of the raids, McGee replied in a public letter.

... this thing you ask cannot be done ... to whatever punishment the law hands him over, no word of mine can ever be spoken in mitigation; not even, under these circumstances, if he were my own brother.[20]

As the election of 1867 approached, McGee began to identify the names of Montreal suspects. He linked local political opposition with Fenianism. The result was to make him anything except popular. He failed to become President of the Montreal St. Patrick's Society, the organisation which had first nominated him in 1857. He was expelled from the society as a member, and its president was nominated to oppose him in the forthcoming election. As McGee's campaign against the Fenians continued, he was replaced in the Canadian government. A letter from the Prime Minister to an Irish Canadian editor gave some indication of the reason. The editor of the *Canadian Freeman* had supported McGee against the Fenians and was now hoping to run as a government candidate. The Prime Minister replied, "... in consequence of your bold and patriotic course in the Fenian matter you have alienated so many of the Catholic laity it would be impossible to elect you".[21] The Premier's reasoning seemed to be justified when McGee failed to be returned for Prescott in the new

19. *Gazette* (Montreal), 19 April 1864.
20. *Christian Guardian,* 27 June 1866.
21. Public Archives of Canada, Moylan Papers, Macdonald to Moylan, 4 July 1867.

Province of Ontario. In McGee's federal constituency of Montreal West, he failed to carry a majority of Irish votes for the first time.

McGee's waning influence with the Irish Catholic voters indicated that his activities alone were not responsible for the reluctance of the Canadian Irish to join the Fenian movement. McGee's opposition to the Fenians cost him his position as the leader of the Canadian Irish. Commenting on McGee's political future, the French Canadian newspaper, *La Minerve*, declared, "C'est certain que M. McGee est 'a dead duck'."[22] The editorial proved to be even more prophetic when McGee was cut down by an assassin's bullet—the only assassination in Canada's history.

Thus, Canadian nationalists seemed justified when they spoke of McGee's Canadian nationalism. However, the one aspect about McGee's opposition to the Fenians that they continually ignored, was that it went far beyond the boundaries of Canada. To McGee, the American Fenians were not only a threat to the Irish in Canada; but Irish republicanism generally was a threat to the future of the Irish nation. His public statements were published in and addressed to Irish and American newspapers, as well as Canadian journals. Private letters to the editors of the *Nation* and the *Canadian Freeman* indicated McGee's concern for the effect of republicanism on Ireland's future.

> . . . we have in the way, the worst obstacle, the devil has ever invented for the Irish, an *irreligious revolutionary society,* in which patriotism takes the garb, of indifferentism, or hostility to religion. This is *the* enemy of the Irish cause in our time; and it is that, every man should combat, *first and foremost.*
>
> . . . it is not honest men, gone astray, that we have to deal with, but dogmatic, anti-clerical demagogues, strong in their pride of opinion and eager for propagandism—a new sect, in fact, who aim at "changing the heart and mind of Ireland" —i.e. the faith and feeling of the people—even more than its government. This sect is altogether novel in Irish history and it is not to be put down, by half apologetic pleadings of "good intentions".[23]

22. Quoted in J. Phelan, *The Ardent Exile,* (Toronto 1951), p. 275.
23. Province of Ontario Archives, McGee to Moylan, 27 October 1865.

The passion and vigour of McGee's opposition to the Irish Republican Brotherhood stemmed less from his concern for local politics or Canadian nationalism, and more from his concern for the Irish future. The sincerity of that concern was evident in the programme he began to outline for Irish reform. During a visit to Wexford in 1865, McGee spoke at a public dinner. He insisted that he had done more, and could continue to do more for the Irish cause as a member of the Canadian government than Irish American nationalists whom he called irresponsible demagogues. The public address created a great controversy when he described his own activities in 1848 as the "follies of one and twenty".[24] In Irish, American and Canadian newspapers, he was denounced for his condemnation of Irish republicanism and the contrast he presented between the Irish in "British and Republican North America". When historians have taken up the controversy, they have ignored one of the speech's principal features. For all his proclaiming of the Canadian experience, McGee argued that Irish immigration was fatal to the Irish national cause. Instead of encouraging the Irish to settle in Canada, he urged them to remain at home and work for the betterment of their country by following the example of Irish Canadians.

Returning to Canada, McGee then began to use what influence he had to urge Irish reform. In letters to Disraeli, Lord Mayo and Lord Kimberley, he called for the appointment of prominent Irishmen to a Royal Commission to investigate the Irish situation. While he claimed that he would not presume to dictate what the policy for Ireland should be, he reminded the British officials of the Canadian experience and the Irish in Canada.

> We have here no established Church, no system of tenancy at will, no poor laws, nor any need of them. We have instead, complete religious equality among all our Churches, a general acquisition of property as the reward of well-directed industry, the fullest local control of our own resources and revenues; our collegiate and primary education; our public works, our militia, marine and courts of justice. Therefore it is, my Lord,

24. Quoted in D. C. Lyne, *The Irish in the Province of Canada in the Decade Leading up to Confederation,* unpublished M.A. thesis, McGill, 1957, Appendix "C".

we are loyal to the Queen in Canada ... Were it otherwise, we would be otherwise.[25]

While it is impossible to assess the effect of McGee's opinion on British policy, it can be noted that both Lord Mayo and Gladstone referred to McGee's arguments in the debates on Land Reform and Disestablishment.

McGee's opposition to the Fenians in Canada, the United States and Ireland emanated from his own sense of Irish patriotism. Even though one might consider McGee's patriotism to have been misdirected, one cannot deny that he was a patriot of the first rank. His patriotism had its origins in the Ireland of his youth and was manifest in his activity with Young Ireland. It gave to the United States a significant immigrant leader and publicist; and to Canada, perhaps her most articulate nationalist. While that patriotism acted in the American environment, McGee's outlook was profoundly shaped by American conditions. Encountering republicanism in the United States, he re-assessed its significance as a solution for Irish difficulties, and came to a new sense of Irish history and destiny. The Canadian experience confirmed his developing conservatism, and convinced him that the solution offered by the Irish Republican Brotherhood would be fatal to Irish unity and nationality.

Finally, McGee's opposition to Fenianism raises some questions to one who is a novice in Irish and American history. If the American environment worked to make Irish American nationalists more radical, could it not also operate to make some more conservative? Does the conservatism of the Catholic Church in the United States stem as much from the American environment as from the traditionalism of its philosophy? Did the American Church influence the direction of the Irish Church in the way that Irish American nationalists influenced the direction of Irish reform? Does not McGee's career indicate the importance of the Canadian experience as an alternative with which to critically evaluate the Irish and American experiences through comparative analysis? Is not the Canadian experience of the Irish significant for Irish and American history? It was McGee who wrote :

25. Public Archives of Canada, John O'Gorman Papers, McGee to Lord Mayo, 5 April 1868.

One in name and in fame
Are the sea-divided Gaels.[26]

Surely the legitimacy of that hypothesis for historians extends the frontiers of Irish and American history to Canada.

26. T. D. McGee, *The Poems of Thomas D'Arcy McGee,* M. A. Sadlier ed. (New York 1868).

FENIANISM IN THE CONTEXT OF WORLD HISTORY

MICHAEL HURST

FEW men have the intellectual inclination and mental discipline
to make the effort necessary for judging what is going on about
them with anything approaching objectivity. In Ireland the past has
a habit of being part and parcel of the present and what might
have been got into perspective through genuinely historical treatment often remains inextricably intertwined with political, social or
economic passion long after any practical importance it possessed
has passed away. Understanding Irish history is therefore often
just as difficult for Irishmen, whether north or south of the border,
as understanding the contemporary scene. And the dispassionate
historian generally battles in vain to set the record straight, for
the audience he suits is select and its influence over the populace
in this particular comparatively limited. Even in the strictly Irish
context then the true significance of the great movements of the
past often remains somewhat clouded. Fenianism has certainly been
surrounded by an aura of romanticism and any place it may have
had outside the Irish parish in a United Kingdom or world
setting largely ignored.

Only through an understanding of its proper place in Irish
history, of course, can a foundation be laid for building any views
about these wider matters. That 1867 should be selected out at all
as the most notable year for Fenianism is in itself a strong indication of how much explaining there is to do. The choice emphasises
the allegedly glorious military side of the story, whereas in fact
the more sustained and less obtrusive aspects of Fenian activity
were the truly influential ones. Were the "organisation" (the name
generally employed by supporters) to be judged upon the basis
of the near ludicrous insurrection of March 1867, it would deserve
to be bracketed with the forces behind the ill-fated Emmet in
1803. But a rebellion, while not to be dismissed lightly in any
circumstances, is not always the whole story and the preventive
measures taken by the government had had a more stifling tem-
porary effect in 1867 than those of 1798. So despite the wider
incidence and deeper intensity of conflict in the earlier outbreak,

what mattered more was the emotional drive and organisational solidity mustered by the Fenians behind the scenes. The leaders of 1798, and indeed those of the comparatively minor affray of 1848, found that collapse of their cause came in the wake of military disaster. Not so O'Mahony, Stephens and their like. The "organisation" remained virtually intact and in some respects went from strength to strength, rivalling, spurring on, or actively working with the constitutional side of Irish nationalism. Certainly 1798 did not lack consequences. The foundation of the United Kingdom, however, was a very different proposition from the wide range of legislation passed at Westminster in the hope of stifling Fenianism.

At the end of the Grattan period Ireland had yet to experience any truly national "green" political parties of the type founded and led by O'Connell for the Emancipation and Repeal causes. The overall framework round which a defeated nationalist group could rally simply did not exist. Though 1848 came at a time when Dublin-led popular "green" politics had become a commonplace, it was scarcely more than a desperate demonstration of the parlous condition into which the national cause had fallen under the terrible impact of the "great famine". In fact the Fenian movement was founded and run largely by men initiated into active rebellion by Young Ireland during the "year of revolutions". It represented nationalist revival and consolidation. Nor could the damp squib of a rebellion be taken to mean that nine years of tireless labour for throwing off the British connection and Ascendancy rule had been spent in vain. Cardinal Cullen's bid to replace revolution with constitutionalism through the National Association came to nothing. Although the main purpose of O'Mahony and Stephens was and remained thwarted and a series of piecemeal reforms were passed, Fenianism kept the minds of a substantial section of the Irish Catholic peasant and urban masses firmly fixed on the notion of national liberation as a general panacea. Fenian disavowal of interest in anything beyond it was at least partly disingenuous, for everyone knew that an independent Ireland would entail the displacement of the Protestant-dominated landlord class and the advent of peasant land owning. In a predominantly agricultural country such an understanding, albeit often unspoken, served as a powerful wind in the sails of national self-assertion. To date the proper union of the political and land issues from the "New

Course" arrangements made between Davitt, Devoy and Parnell confuses the issue and ignores a most fundamental feature of Irish nationalism. Deliberately or not, Fenianism, like the Repeal party earlier on, flourished as an organisation because it struck the populace as a fine catalyst for all the underdog conflict groupings—political, social and economic—constituted by their activist sections. Many a pronouncement from the head hid the realities of the heart. After the destruction of the native or nativised Catholic ruling class by "reconstruction" the peasantry had become the sole lasting repository of a separate Irish national consciousness linked to the desire for political independence. For it land and nationality were indestructibly linked and any bid for national self-rule bereft of landowning connotations would have been meaningless.

All this is not to say the defeat of 1867 was without vital effects in the movement. Far from it. Both the timely official anticipation of trouble and the subsequent humiliations of defeat and imprisonment produced a more sober and realistic mood at all levels of Fenian activity. Readiness to stand aside and let a moderate constitutionalist like Butt go ahead with something as limited as a genuinely-felt Federalism proved that. There was, curiously, a personal element present. As defence counsel for Fenian prisoners and the leader of an agitation for their pardon and release, Butt had rapidly built up a substantial reserve of goodwill in "organisation" circles which only faulty execution of parliamentary warfare destroyed. And it is the point of faulty execution that needs emphasis, for no full-scale reversion to pre-rebellion violence followed upon the disillusionment about Butt—just another experiment with a new-type parliamentarian. Before this man—Parnell—acquired a firm mastery over Irish nationalism generally, Fenianism was one of the important elements to be assuaged in the power game. Like the Roman Catholic hierarchy it had to be handled with kid gloves. The "New Departure" from a Fenian viewpoint was a move putting Parnell in as a probationer. From his viewpoint it was the first step towards his capturing the allegiance of the nationalist left. Very much as Gladstone had earlier taken command of the various Liberal sections and welded them into a mighty political unity, Parnell gradually relegated Fenianism to the level of ana djunct. But it remained one that demanded constant courting and always posed a danger to his control. When the delays and intricacies of the parliamentary game grew irksome to the impatient sections of a sorely tried people Fenianism always reacted sharply and served as a potential rallying point for the frustrated and hard-pressed. Ironically enough though, Parnell still dominated the left in the time of his disgrace, but only by willy nilly adopting an out and out anti-British line backed by strong revolutionary overtones. With his death things changed and the rather sickly left was once again open to the pull of Fenianism—or rather what remained of it. Satisfaction of numerous economic and social grievances, coupled with a partial amelioration of economic conditions played into moderate hands. Fresh intellectual developments led to the emergence of the Sinn Fein and cultural revival movements. Yet the old "organisation" lingered on and new groups of dedicated young men cast older, corrupted and disillusioned ones aside. In Easter Week 1916 it was the Fenians who provided the backbone of the direct action "Boys". And here came a defeat which led to the recreation of mass support for the extreme position. 1867 had not been undone—simply replaced. Replaced by a symbol of quite glorious failure and a rallying cry which served to drive nationalist Ireland on to shame the British into making major concessions. Needless to say, such successes as the Fenians had, early or late, owed a lot to the nature of British strengths and weaknesses. Nevertheless, the persistence and moral courage of their following at crucial times was considerable—quite sufficient to dispose of the argument that without assitance from the U.S.A. the movement would have fallen apart. Extreme elements of Irish Americans had undoubtedly set it on its feet and poured in much needed money at frequent intervals. Money alone, however, is hardly a force in politics at all unless the emotional climate for its use is relatively favourable. The heartfelt cravings of the Irish Catholic masses made just such a climate and progress was assured.

Fenianism was a mass-backed phenomenon, run on a semi-secret basis and dedicated to the overthrow of British rule. Both its extreme political ends and violence of approach alienated the Catholic Church, the more so because of the oaths and secrecy associated with them. It would be a mistake to assume because of this that the movement was anti-clerical. No extremist priest was ever turned from its doors. Rather it would be true to say that it shared in common with several later versions of extreme Irish nationalism the characteristic of being above the whole matter of being anti-clerical or pro-clerical. Nationalism first, second and third was its unwavering order of priorities. In Irish history, therefore, Fenianism formed the basis for the drive to independence at almost all times after its foundation. From it or its work Parnell, Griffith and de Valera drew much valuable support and inspiration. And at the end, when all the sugar had been extracted from the nationalist cane and the treacle and the golden syrup of independence consumed, there remained the dirty molasses of the I.R.A. ready to battle on against Westminster and its "minions" at Stormont. Champions of the original untamed Fenian still exist, but with little work to do and even less support for doing it. Unhappily for the bomb-thrower, Parnell built constitutionalism stronger than he knew and the spirit of Butt and Redmond has taken charge in quieter times.

For the British, Fenianism was but Ribbonism plus Young Ireland writ large. Something alien to their notions of domestic government and yet another proof of the tiresome restless petulance of the Catholic Irish. Such was the ignorance and smugness of most sections of active British opinion that rejection of United Kingdom values and the desire to set up a separate Irish state seemed to stray beyond treason into madness. Acts of violence gave an enormous fillip to the already powerful anti-Hibernianism nurtured by history and immigration and those who were not swept along in it tended more often than not to stress the wrongs done to Ireland in the same ways as many of them were doing the wrongs done to factory workers. They saw the Irish Catholic masses as a group of underdogs within a United Kingdom context and scarcely for a moment realised that what was happening over the Irish Sea should have been put into the same category as contemporaneous developments on the continent. After all, it seemed most unreasonable to most of them that anyone in the British Isles should not wish to be part of the most considerable and civilised nation on earth. The notion that had they been alive in 1800 many Irishmen would never have wished to join it at all appeared to some a mere fabrication of wicked men across the Atlantic—men who had been foolish themselves and

were in their spite wishing to drag others down as well. Even those
of the most sophisticated school of thought among the reformers,
who were willing to admit the Union might have been unnecessary,
tended to argue that the best possible thing for the future was to
make it work and raise Ireland to British levels. Scotland and
Wales were different from England and parts of England showed
distinct regional variations. Could not Irish feelings be accom-
modated within the United Kingdom framework in the same way,
provided the Irish majority was allowed its rightful influence? So
ran the argument of the "enlightened" British, or rather the over-
whelming majority of them, for there was almost always a small
section which recognised the notion of Irish political nationality
as legitimate. When Gladstone joined this select band he naturally
reinforced the ascendancy Parnell had established over the physical
force Fenians and while giving much of what Home Rulers
generally wanted, stood firmly in the way of the ultimate Fenian
goal and did so to much greater effect than the hosts of Orangeism
or unionist Liberalism. Nor, while Parnell and he were united in
their "hearts" did rejection of Home Rule by the British electorate
leave Fenianism any way through to widespread success.

Great though his feeling for and grasp of nationalism was, even
Gladstone failed to see Ireland in its real context. Here in fact was
a country lacking that very common ground between the different
sections of the community and different political parties which
made it so easy for liberal constitutionalism to operate in Britain
itself. Without British controlled administration and armed forces
the Irish would have been in a constant state of open or partially
open civil war. Ireland was overwhelmingly divided into two
nations—and roughly in the Disraelian sense at that. One was the
"green" nation, the other the "orange". What didn't fall into
either category was of scant significance in any crisis. Before the
substantial widening of the parliamentary franchise for county
constituencies in 1884 the considerable number of non-Home
Rulers sent to Westminster from Irish areas with a Catholic
population seemed to prove nationalism did not command overall
support among the "greenites". There was ample evidence to the
contrary and the widespread support for the Fenians in the years
before Parnell made up a vital element in it. Only with the 1885
general election though did the forces backing Fenianism find wide

expression through the ballot. By strengthening Parnell still more and giving the impression that Irish nationalism had been absorbed into the parliamentary game, this beggared understanding of the real core of the quarrels in Ireland and hid the limited belief in constitutionalism to be found on both sides. With the Lords' veto gone and Home Rule impending, first the "orange" then the "green" party swung round to open espousal of force in the period immediately before the First World War. Developments like these, involving the abandonment of Westminster "manners", were frequently to be seen in inter-war Europe in countries with social structures similar in fundamentals to the Irish. The junior partner of the United Kingdom was not a solid nation-state of the sort found in western and northern Europe. She had much more in common with the unhappy congeries of peoples in the centre, east and south-east of the continent. In short, Ireland within the British context was a strongly foreign element, despite numerous shared features both profound and superficial. It was as though an African had dressed in European clothes and claimed he was therefore a European. As a lasting element in Irish politics Fenianism emphasised this point.

This clear, the broader significance of Fenianism is easier to explain. Many nationalist movements have been set on foot outside the homeland. Some were intended to serve as a spur to those on the spot, but the market in Ireland was ready and waiting for the Fenians. For reasons many of which derived from involvement in the highly sophisticated complex of United Kingdom liberalism, Catholic Ireland developed its democratic politics at a great rate—greater indeed than the one in Britain itself, where class bitterness seldom rose to such dizzy heights. Fenianism therefore began with more than a Carbonari-style mission and had a great deal in common with recent phenomena like the Jewish organisations in Palestine or the Greek Cypriot EOKA. The American base from which it started had only a community connotation. No Louis Napoleon was over in Washington waiting to ask an Irish Cavour what he could do for Ireland. Irish America and Irish America alone was committed to furthering the cause of Irish national independence. Yet in the main the strictly unofficial outside help and moral support from over the Atlantic certainly acted as an enormous encouragement to the Fenians at home in Ireland, faced with the world's largest power and its local governing and colonial representatives whose hands had long controlled the great bulk of the island's wealth. American Jewry's quest to implement Balfour's Declaration of 1917 to the letter and wrest Palestine from the Arabs was on the face of it a much less demanding operation, given the determination of the Zionist settlers and Arab weakness. In the case of Palestine partition between Jews and Arabs was imposed by the Great Powers. In that of Ireland it was imposed by Great Britain against herself as well as against the latter-day Fenians of Sinn Fein. As in the Austro-Hungarian Empire, so in the United Kingdom—agitation, albeit with avowedly treasonable ends, could be carried quite a long way without the imposition ofs trong legal cures. The Fenians would have had to be great duffers not to have made headway among the Catholic Irish under such conditions.

Mazzini used naively to assume that all nations rightly struggling to be free shared a profound feeling of sympathy and mutual compassion. Still more naively he supposed that his own country would be regarded as "The Christ among the nations" because of its long struggle for freedom and the grand lead he had set out to give to the doctrines of nationalism. Strangely enough the Irish nationalists never felt for the "risorgimento" in the same way as the British. It would have been surprising had continental peoples followed Mazzini's ideal, but, being linked with the radicalism of the British, American and French traditions and tucked away from frontier squabbles with fellow aspirants for freedom, the Fenians might have been rated likely potential allies for the Italians. But parochialism will out. One of the less attractive characteristics of the downtrodden is their almost inevitable self-centredness. The Pope was the head of Catholic Christendom. He had therefore to be defended—never mind against who. So thought most Irish Catholics and the small bands of non-clerical leaders could not risk rupture with their rank and file, or lavish hard-won resources from America upon foreigners. Just as the Montenegrins thought of themselves as one with Russia when they cried: "With the Russians we are a hundred millions", the Fenians in Ireland regarded Irish America as just part of the great Irish nation. They were flesh and blood in the fullest sense. The United States was not thought of as a foreign country. Within the Anglo-Saxon world was an unofficial Irish empire and outside it things could go hang, unless someone was up in arms against the British providing scope for an action against a common enemy. Irish sentiment, not liberalism, drove on the Fenians and that fact is strongly and sadly illustrated today by the attitude of Irish America generally towards the negroes. Under the influence of constitutional liberalism the majority of Irish nationalists in Ireland gradually embraced a wider outlook and largely threw off the parochialism which conditions over the Atlantic only served to perpetuate into our own day. This common concern for justice and liberty everywhere held sway in all but the most extreme manifestations of the Fenian spirit during the final struggles for Irish independence. Latterly clericalism and unquenched hatred of the British have sometimes brought Irish militants to the side of some very illiberal causes. Nonetheless, Fenianism and the bulk of its concomitants and successors in Ireland belong mostly to the radical nationalist school of politics. Realisation of their basic aim led to disunity. Most of the factions opted for liberal constitutionalism and sought to recover the "Six Counties" by diplomacy. The molasses fought on. Are liberals cynical realists or honest men upholding the true spirit of Fenianism in a nonparochial way? Fenianism wanted to fight but often changed its methods. Are diplomacy and accommodation no more than "dirty" betrayal? Are the bitter-enders the real idealists, or blind fools defeating their own ends? Ireland is not yet far enough from 1867 for generally acceptable answers to be given to these questions. One thing, however, is beyond dispute. Fenianism contributed much to both the ploughshare and the sword notions of Irish nationalism. Peace through war and war through peace had places in its diverse and practical philosophy.